CORNER
&
BORDER

DESIGNS

ECKEN *&* REIHEN
ANGULOS *&* ORLAS
COINS *&* BORDURES
ANGOLI *&* ORLI

1900

CORNER
&
BORDER
DESIGNS

ECKEN *&* REIHEN
ANGULOS *&* ORLAS
COINS *&* BORDURES
ANGOLI *&* ORLI

1900

THE PEPIN PRESS

Copyright for this edition
© 1996, 1998 The Pepin Press B/v

First published in 1996 by The Pepin Press
Reprinted in 1998

Copyright introduction 'Border & Corner Designs 1900'
© 1996, 1998 Pepin Van Roojen

ISBN 90 5496 012 4

The Pepin Press
POB 10349 • 1001 EH Amsterdam • The Netherlands
Tel (+) 31 20 4202021 • Fax (+) 31 20 4201152 • e-mail: pepin@euronet.nl
Printed in Singapore

Border & Corner Designs 1900

As with general ornaments used to embellish printed materials in the late nineteenth and early twentieth century, the design of border and corner motifs from this period can be traced to a variety of sources, notably Renaissance, Baroque, and Gothic styles. However, also recognizable are patterns based on ancient Greco-Roman or Egyptian motifs. Other derivations were from Celtic, Arabic and Turkish origins, the latter in the form of geometrical motifs based on stylised floral compositions. Shapes inspired by the decorative arts of the Far East form a distinct group, characterized by rounded and swirling curves based on organic themes, such as the flow of water and coiling vegetation. These latter were also of great influence on the emergence of Art Nouveau, the principal new European style of the turn of the twentieth century.

Many type foundries produced border material to be used with specific typefaces popular at the time, such as Baskerville, Bodoni, Caslon, Garamond, etc. Considered very modern were ornaments built of dots, triangles and squares, or shaded and wavy lines, mostly to be combined with sans serif typefaces.

Most of the designs shown in this book demonstrate their adaptability to the printing technique for mass reproduction of the time, for which lead or copper settings were used. Border designs were available in the form of matrices of various lengths, with matching corner pieces, providing almost unlimited possibilities for typographic decoration. Also, border material could be combined, and designs made more complex, resulting in multiple borders, sometimes with further decorations in the corners. Around 1900, typesetters were, in effect, also designers, as the decisions which decorative material to be used with texts were often up to them. The many decorative possibilities and styles, created a rich and resourceful graphic design environment, and the many illustrations in this book form an enormous wealth of information for modern designers.

Rand- und Eckverzierungen um 1900

Wie alle Ornamentik des ausgehenden 19. und beginnenden 20. Jahrhunderts entspringen die Formen der Rand- und Eckmotive, mit denen die Druckerzeugnisse dieser Zeit häufig verziert wurden, vielen verschiedenen Stilepochen, vor allem aber der Renaissance, dem Barock und der Gotik. Man kann zudem Motive finden, die ihren Ursprung in alten griechisch-römischen oder ägyptischen Quellen haben. Ebenso gibt es Ornamente, die sich an keltische, arabische und türkische Vorbilder anlehnen. Die türkischen Motive sind an ihren geometrischen, stilisierten floralen Kompositionen zu erkennen – Formen, die auf der dekorativen Kunst des Fernen Ostens beruhen und sich durch ihre runde, geschwungene Linienführung auszeichnen, in der sich fließendes Wasser und vegetabilischer Schwung erkennen lassen. Diese Formen hatten einen großen Einfluß auf den sich um die Jahrhundertwende entwickelnden Jugendstil, eine neue Strömung, die in verschiedenerlei Ausprägung ganz Europa erfaßte.

Viele Schriftgießereien fertigten Druckvorlagen für Randleisten an, die zusammen mit den damals gängigen Schrifttypen Baskerville, Bodoni, Caslon, Garamond usw. Verwendung fanden. Zu jener Zeit waren Ornamente beliebt, die sich aus Punkten, Drei- und Vierecken zusammensetzen sowie aus Schraffuren und Wellenlinien. Meistenteils wurden sie mit serifenlosen Schrifttypen kombiniert.

Der Großteil der in diesem Band abgebildeten Entwürfe, für die Blei- oder Kupfersätze verwendet wurden, belegen ihre gute Eignung für die Drucktechniken der Massenproduktion dieser Epoche. In jener Zeit waren die Setzer im Grunde gleichzeitig Entwerfer, da die Entscheidung über die den Text begleitenden Dekorationen gewöhnlich in ihren Händen lag.

Die Randverzierungen gab es als Matrizen unterschiedlicher Länge mit den dazugehörigen Eckstücken. Sie sorgten für schier unendliche typographische Variationsmöglichkeiten. Die einzelnen Randleisten konnten außerdem miteinander kombiniert werden. Dadurch wurden die Formen komplexer, und es entstanden Mehrfachränder, die oft mit weiteren Verzierungen in den Ecken ausgestaltet wurden. Die vielfältigen dekorativen Möglichkeiten und Stile entwickelten sich zu einer reichen und phantasievollen Gebrauchsgraphik. Die vielen Beispiele, die in diesem Band zusammengetragen wurden, sind dazu gedacht, Graphikern unserer Zeit als nützliche Informationsquelle zu dienen.

Motifs pour encadrements et coins 1900

Tout comme les éléments décoratifs généraux utilisés pour embellir les imprimés à la fin du dix-neuvième siècle et au début du vingtième, il est possible de faire remonter les motifs utilisés pour les encadrements et les coins au cours de cette période à diverses sources en particulier, les styles Renaissance, Baroque et Gothique. Cependant, on peut également reconnaître l'inspiration d'anciens motifs gréco-romains ou égyptiens. D'autres motifs sont dérivés d'origines celtiques, arabes et turques, ces dernières sous forme de motifs géométriques basés sur des compositions florales stylisées. Les formes qui sont inspirées des arts décoratifs d'Extrême-Orient forment un groupe à part et sont caractérisées par des courbes arrondies et des volutes basées sur des thèmes organiques comme l'eau qui coule et la végétation ondoyante. Ceux-ci ont eu aussi une grande influence dans l'émergence du style Art Nouveau qui fut le principal style européen nouveau du début du vingtième siècle.

De nombreux fondeurs typographes produisaient des encadrements à utiliser avec des polices de caractères spécifiques très prisées à l'époque telles que Baskerville, Bodoni, Caslon, Garamond, etc. Des motifs formés de points, de triangles et de carrés ou de lignes ombrées ou ondulées étaient considérés comme très modernes à l'époque et étaient principalement alliés à des polices de caractère sans sérif. La plupart des motifs présentés dans ce livre montrent leur adaptabilité aux techniques d'impression en série de l'époque qui utilisaient la composition au plomb ou au cuivre. A cette époque, les compositeurs étaient en fait également des concepteurs car c'était généralement eux qui décidaient quel motif décoratif utiliser avec les différents textes. Les différents styles d'encadrement étaient disponibles sous forme de matrices de diverses longueurs avec coins assortis, fournissant des possibilités de décoration typographique pratiquement illimitées. De plus les encadrements pouvaient être mélangés et les motifs pouvaient être rendus plus complexes, ce qui donnait des encadrements multiples présentant parfois des décorations supplémentaires dans les coins. Les nombreuses possibilités et styles décoratifs créaient un environnement de conception graphique riche et ingénieux et les nombreuses illustrations présentées dans ce livre offrent une mine d'informations précieuse pour les concepteurs modernes.

Decorazioni per i margini e gli angoli 1900

Al pari delle ornamentazioni usate in generale per abbellire il materiale a stampa tra la fine dell'Ottocento e l'inizio del Novecento, il design dei motivi per i margini e gli angoli che risalgono a questo periodo può derivare da varie fonti, specialmente dagli stili rinascimentale, barocco e gotico. Tuttavia sono anche riconoscibili delle decorazioni che si basano su motivi greco-romani o egizi. Altre ancora avevano origini celtiche, arabe e turche, queste ultime in forma di motivi geometrici basati su composizioni floreali stilizzate. Le forme che s'ispiravano alle arti decorative dell'Estremo Oriente fanno gruppo a sé, caratterizzate come sono da curve arrotondate e vorticose basate su temi organici, come il flusso dell'acqua e la vegetazione a volute. Queste ultime forme esercitarono anche una grande influenza sull'allora emergente liberty, la principale novità in fatto di stile nell'Europa a cavallo del secolo. Molte fonderie di caratteri tipografici produssero del materiale per i margini da usare con particolari caratteri popolari in quel tempo, come il Baskerville, il Bodoni, il Caslon, il Garamond, ecc. Molto moderni venivano considerati in quel periodo i motivi ornamentali fatti di punti, triangoli e quadrati, o da linee sfumate e ondulate, che venivano prevalentemente unite a caratteri senza terminazione.

La maggior parte delle decorazioni presentate in questo libro dimostrano la loro adattabilità alla tecnica di stampa per la riproduzione di massa dell'epoca, per cui venivano usate composizioni in piombo o in rame. In questo periodo i compositori erano in effetti anche dei designer, dato che le decisioni sul materiale da usare per le decorazioni dei testi venivano di solito prese da loro.

Le decorazioni dei margini erano disponibili in forma di matrici di varia lunghezza, con pezzi di forma analoga per gli angoli, e offrivano una gamma pressoché illimitata di possibilità per la decorazione tipografica. Inoltre, il materiale per i margini poteva venire combinato, e le forme rese più complesse, producendo dei margini multipli, qualche volta con ulteriori decorazioni negli angoli. Le molte possibilità decorative e stilistiche, crearono per il design grafico un ambiente ricco di risorse, e le molte illustrazioni in questo libro rappresentano una messe enorme di informazioni per i moderni designer.

Diseños de Bordes y Esquineras 1900

De la misma manera en que los adornos generales solían usarse para embellecer los materiales impresos en la última parte del siglo diecinueve y la primera parte del siglo veinte, el diseño de los motivos de bordes y esquineras de este período se derivan de una variedad de fuentes, más notables los estilos del Renacimiento, del Barroco y del Gótico. No obstante, se puede reconocer también los patrones basados en motivos antiguos greco-romanos o egipcios. Otras derivaciones vinieron de orígenes célticos, árabes o turcos, estos últimos en la forma de motivos geométricos basados en composiciones florales de forma estilizada. Las formas inspiradas por las artes decorativas del lejano oriente forman un grupo distinto, caracterizado por curvas redondeadas y arremolinadas, basadas en temas orgánicos, tales como el flujo del agua y el enroscado de la vegetación. Estos últimos también tuvieron un efecto importante sobre el surgimiento del estilo Art Nouveau, el principal estilo nuevo de Europa al principio del siglo veinte.

Muchas fundiciones de tipos producían materiales de borde para uso con los tipos específicos que eran populares en esa época, tales como Baskerville, Bodoni, Caslon, Garamond, etc. Considerados como muy modernos en ese entonces eran los ornamentos fabricados de puntos, triángulos y cuadros, o líneas sombreadas y ondeadas, en la mayoría combinadas con tipos 'sans serif'.

La mayoría de los diseños en este libro demuestran su adaptabilidad a la técnica de impresión para la reproducción en grandes cantidades que se realizaba en esa época, para la cual se usaban composiciones tipográficas de plomo o cobre. Los compositores tipográficos eran, efectivamente, diseñadores también, en vista de que la decisión en cuanto al material decorativo que se iba a usar dependía normalmente de ellos.

Los diseños de bordes estaban disponibles en la forma de matrices de varias longitudes, con esquineras que se empataban con ellas, ofreciendo así posibilidades casi sin límite de diseños tipográficos. Asimismo los materiales de borde podían ser combinados y los diseños hechos más complejos, resultando en bordes múltiples a veces con decoraciones adicionales en las esquinas. Las muchas posibilidades y estilos decorativos, crearon un lujoso e ingenioso ambiente de diseño gráfico, y las muchas ilustraciones en este libro forman una enorme riqueza de información para el diseñador moderno.

BORDER MATRICES

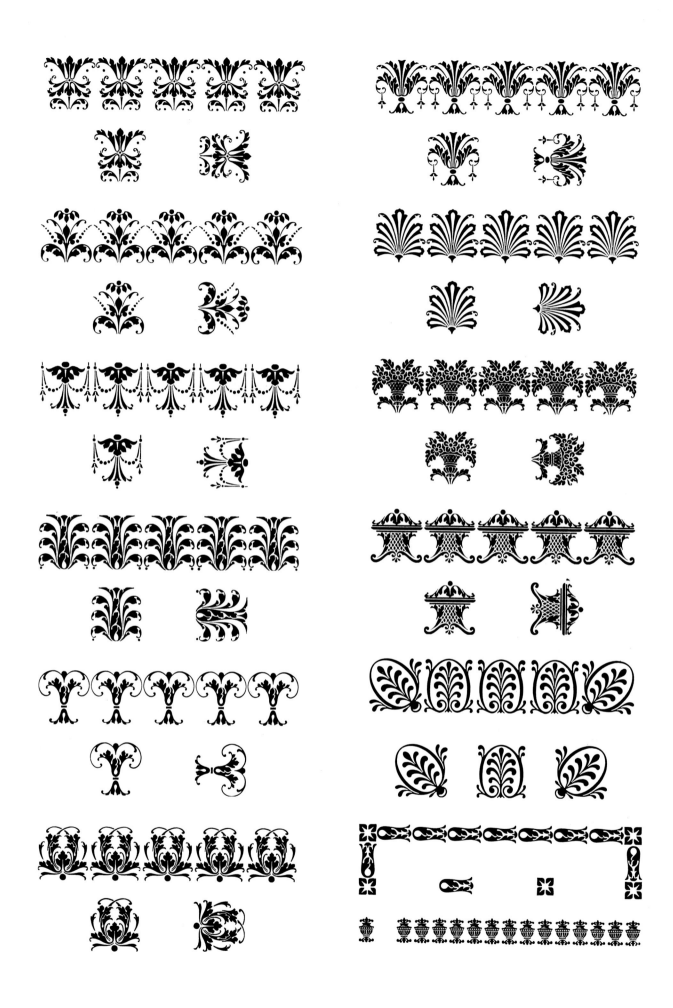

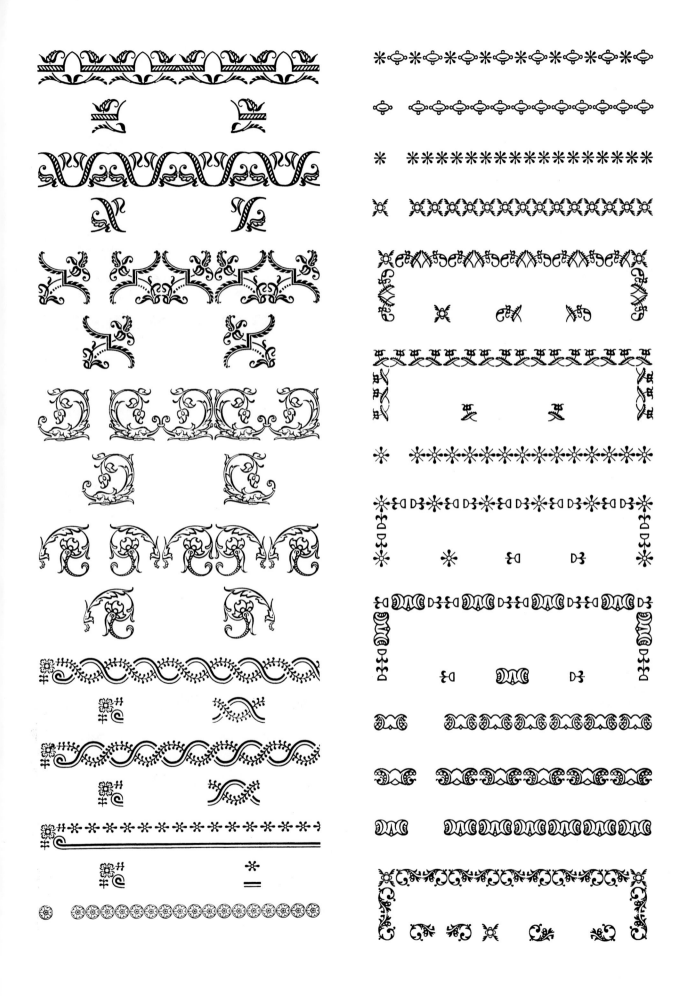

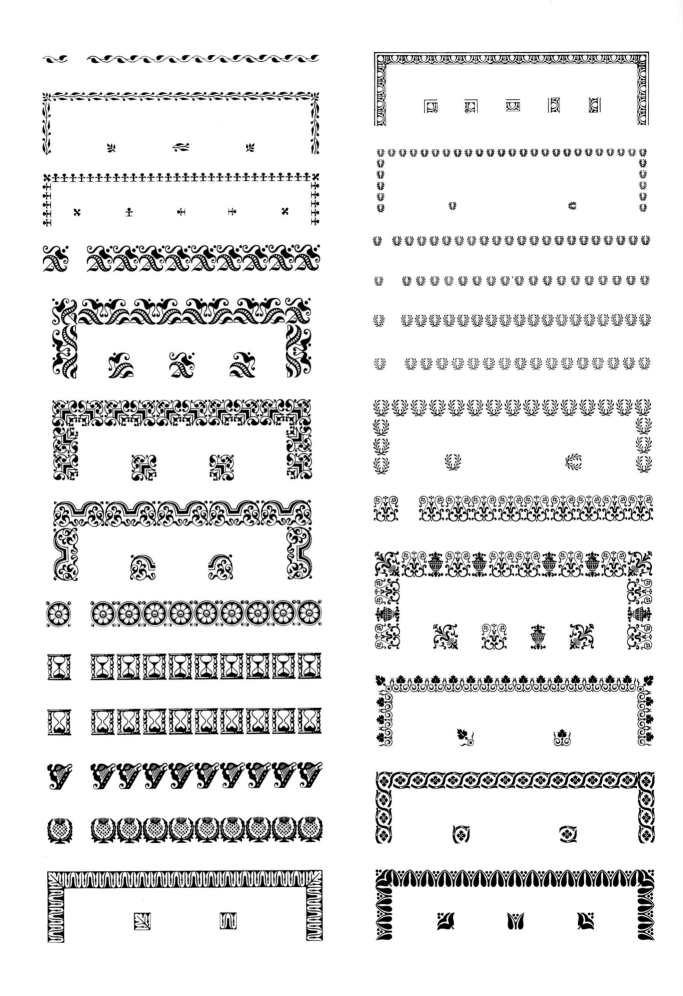

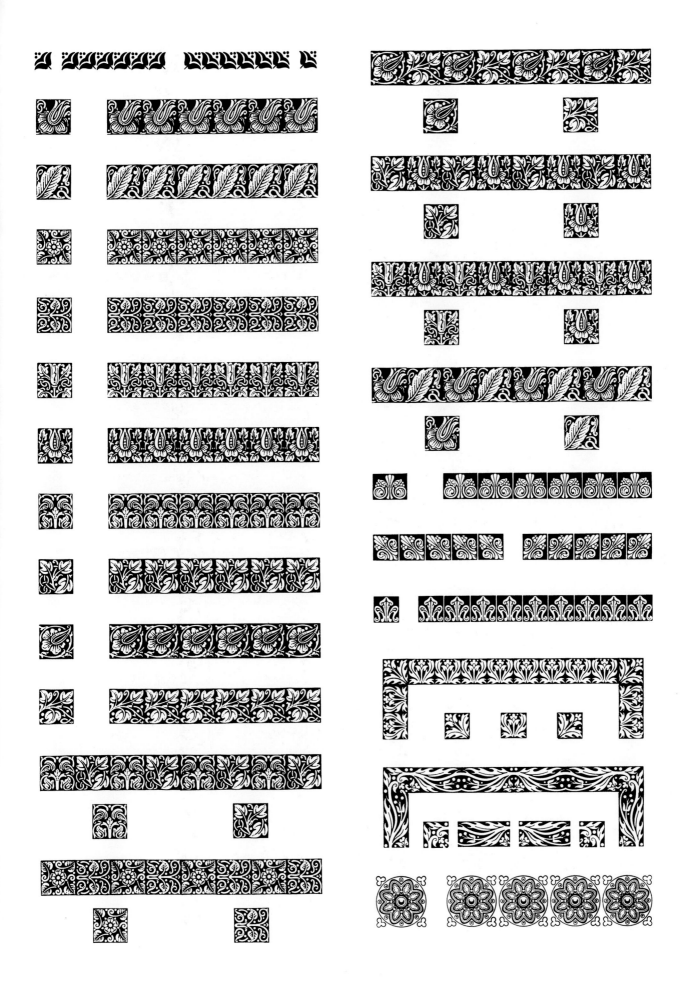

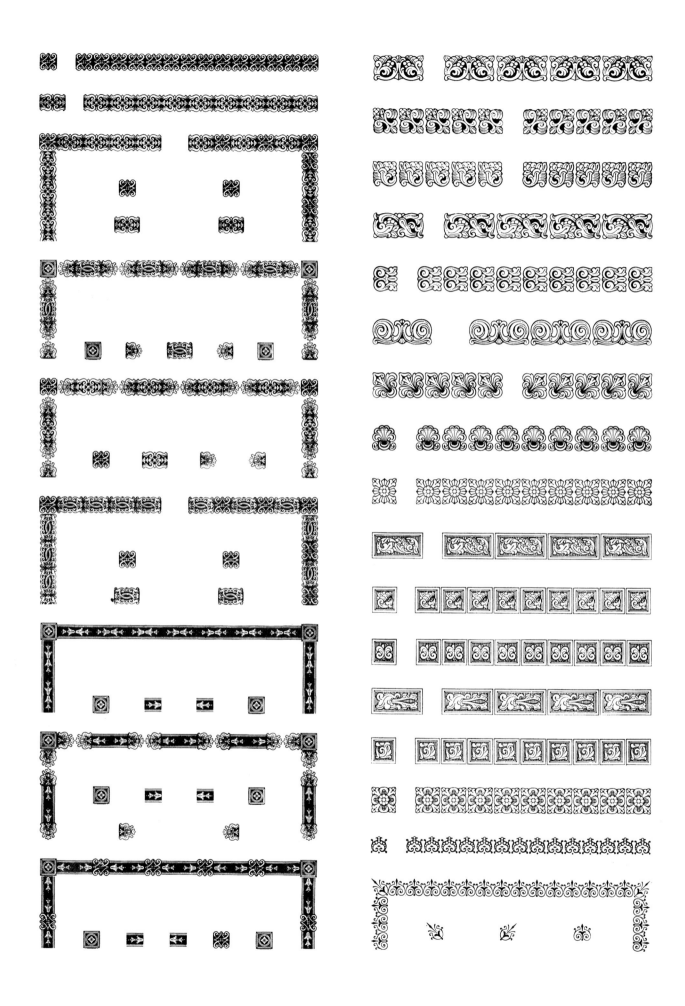

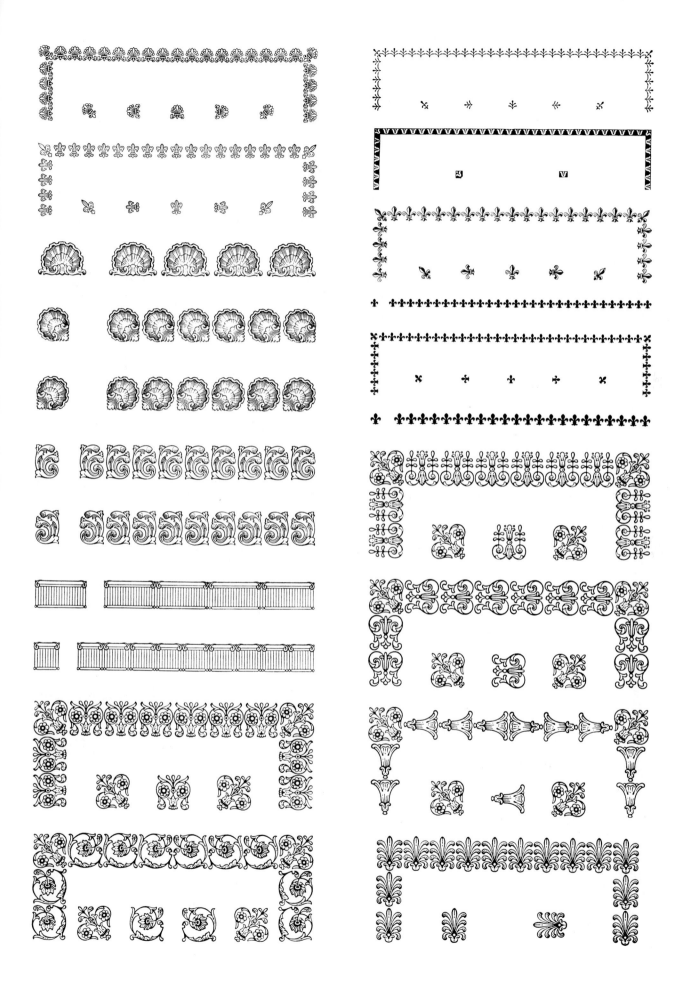

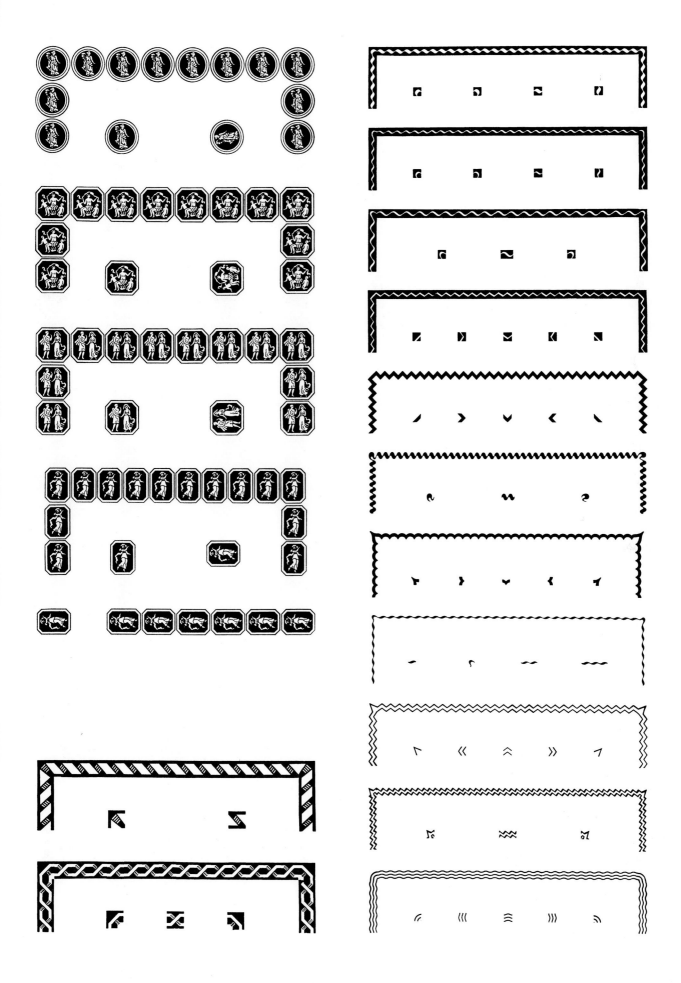

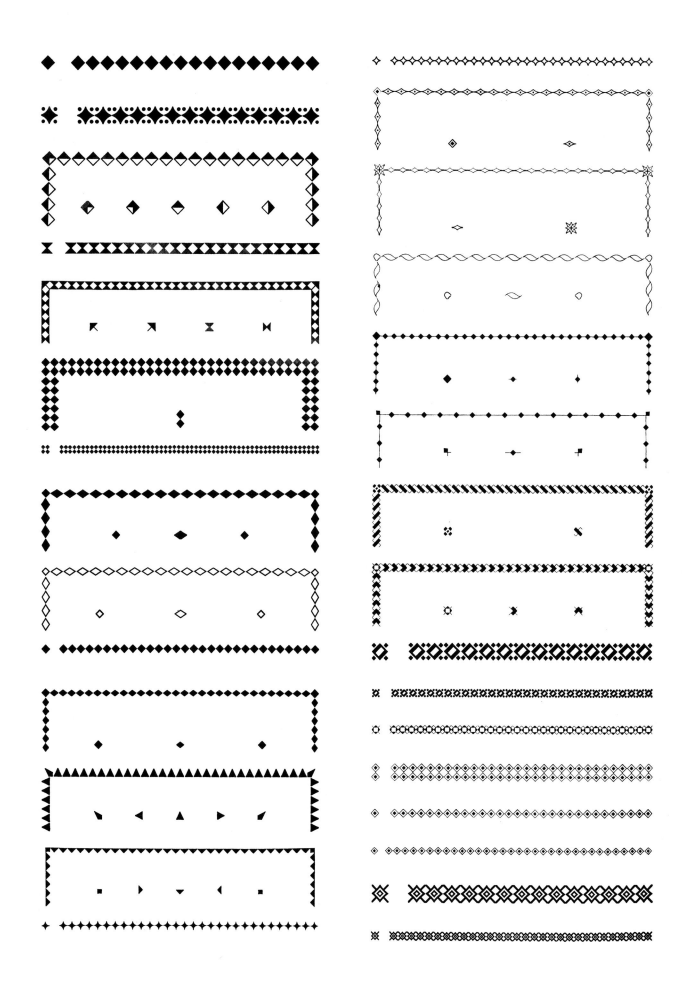

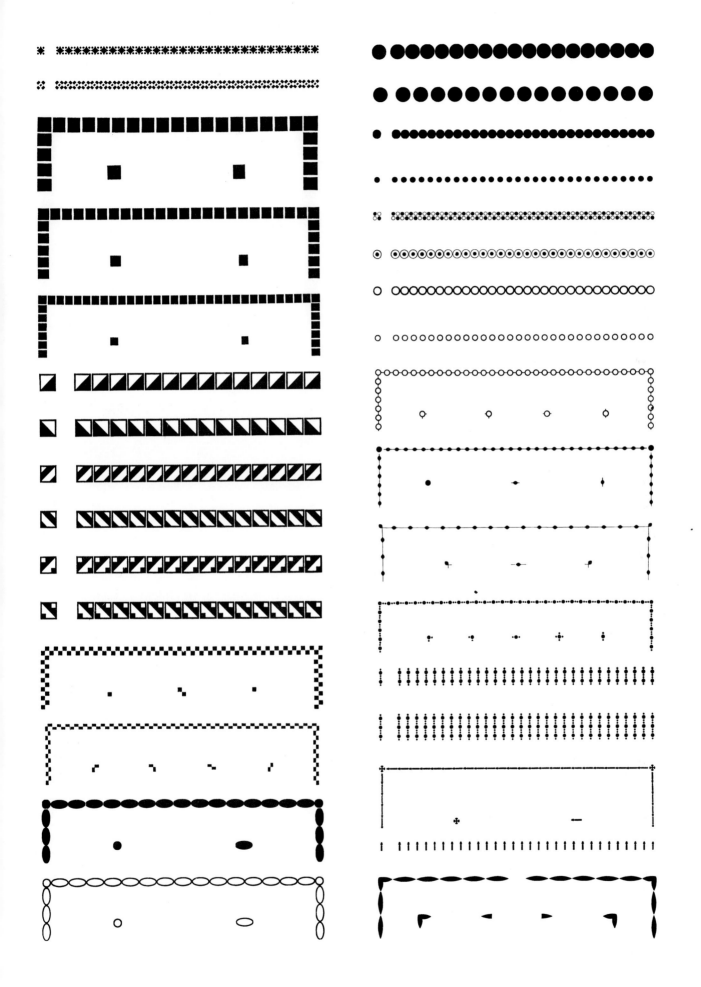

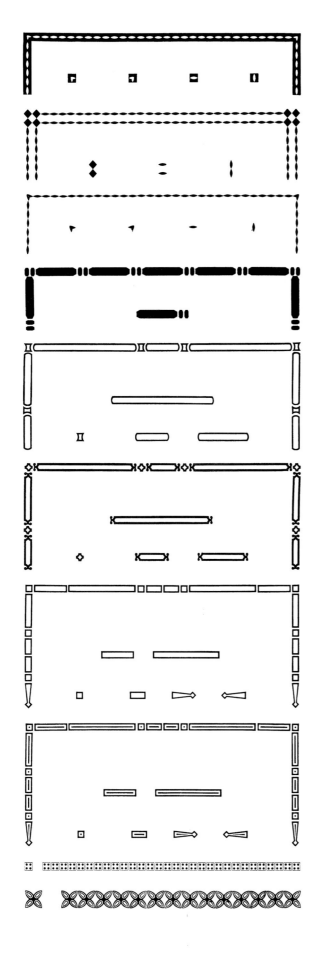

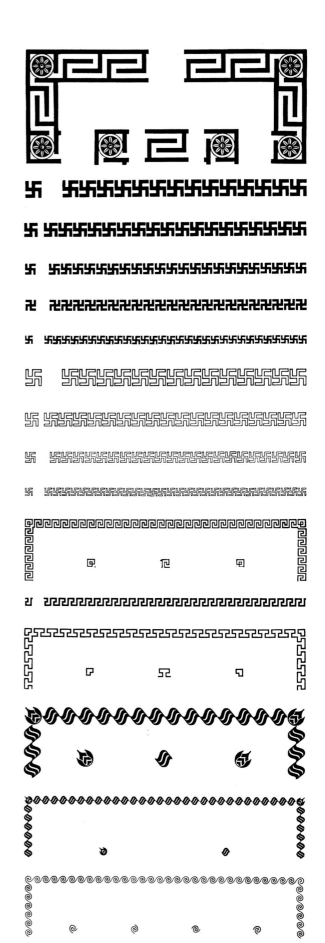

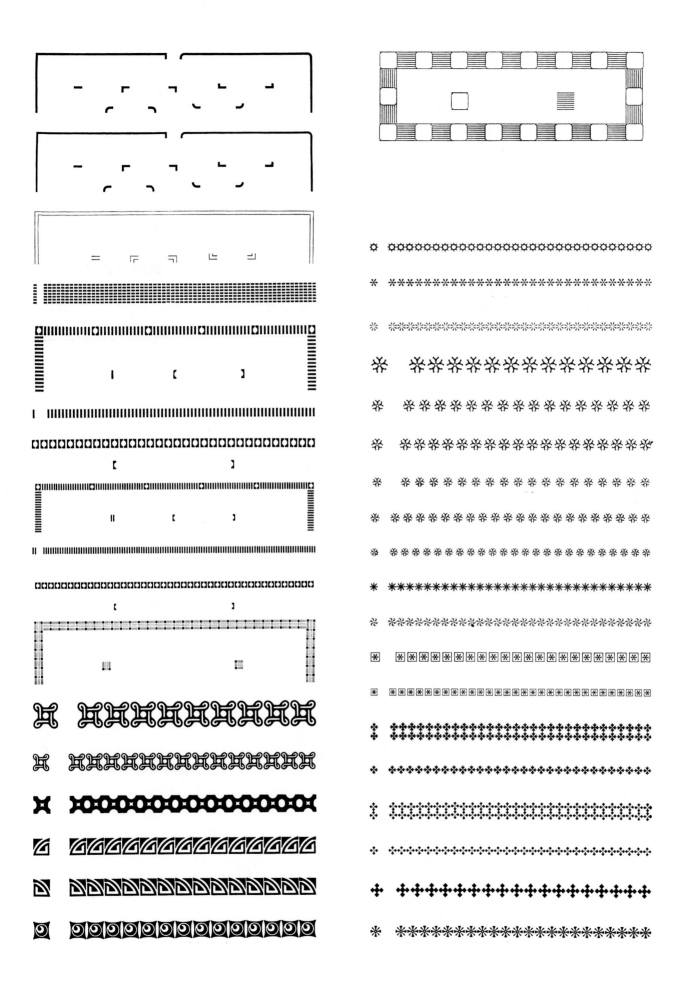

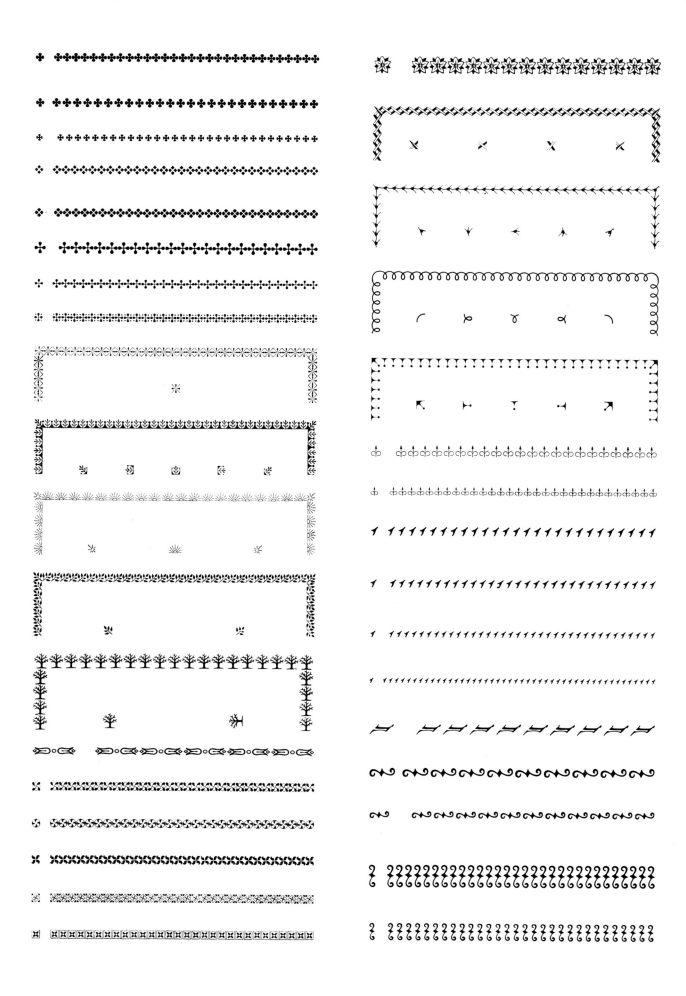

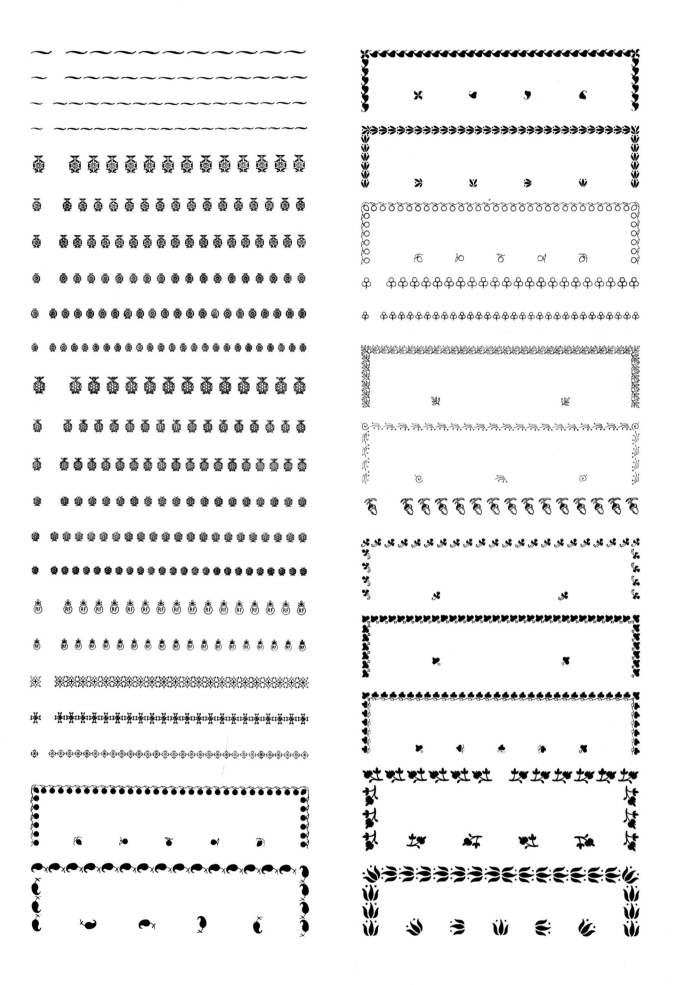

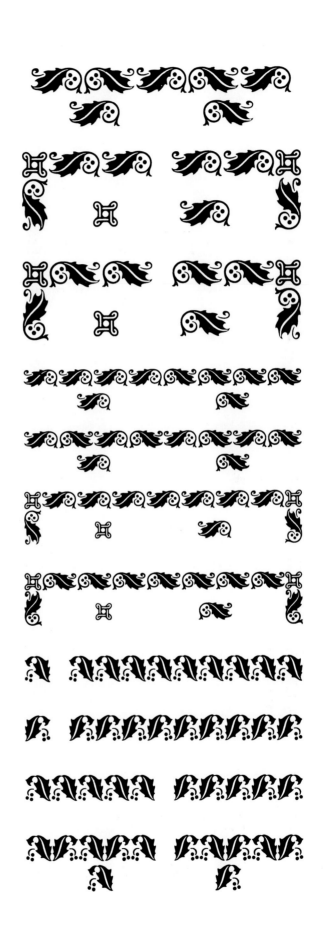

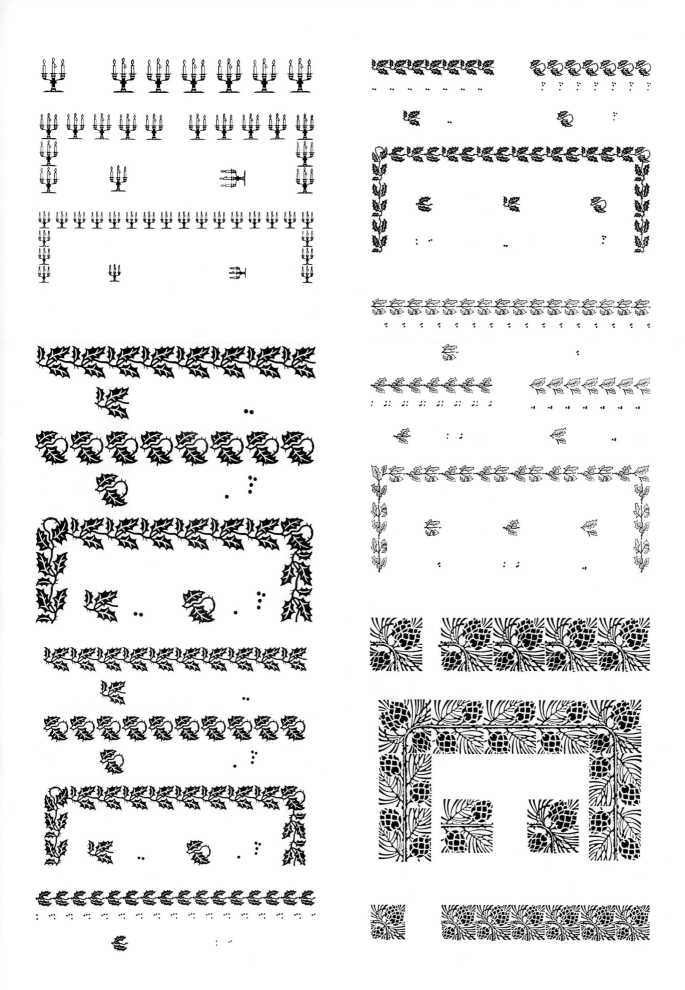

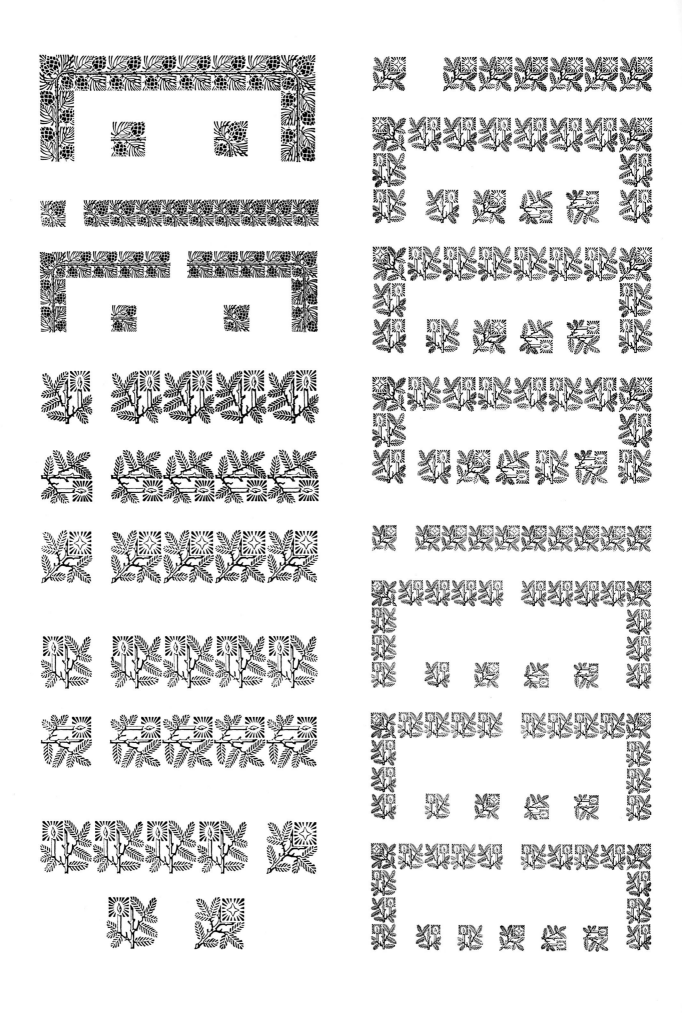

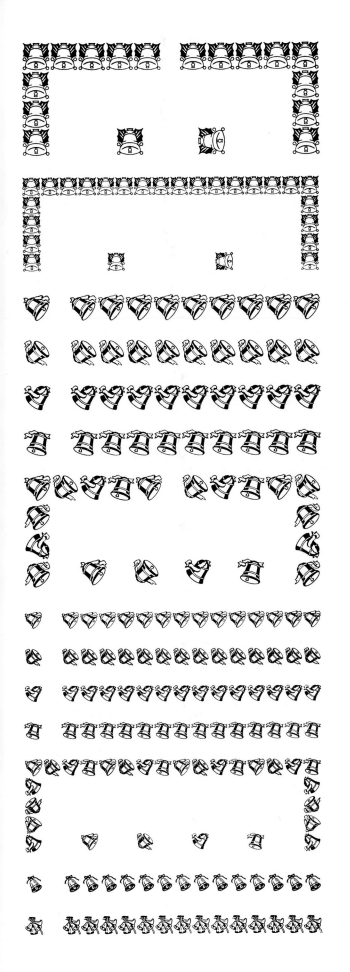

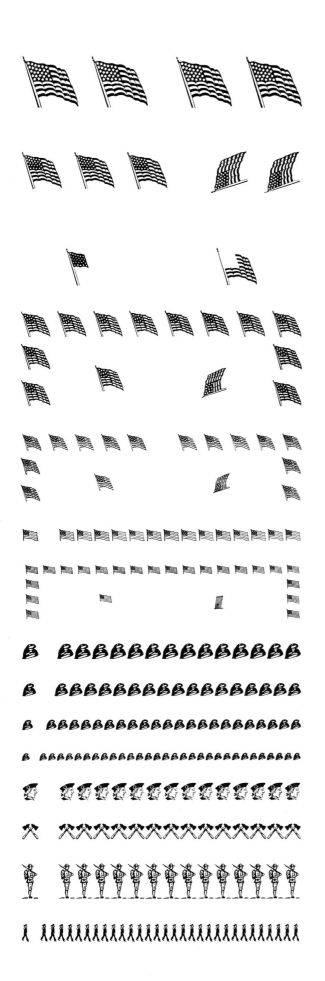

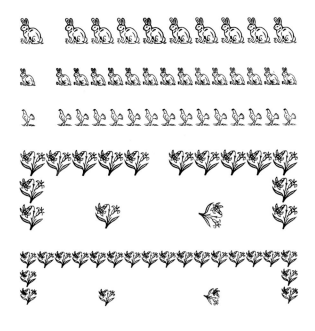

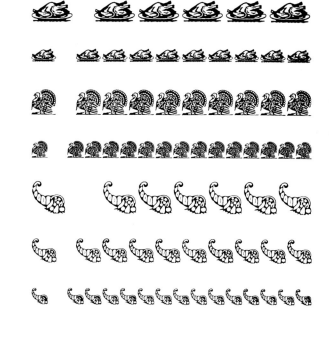

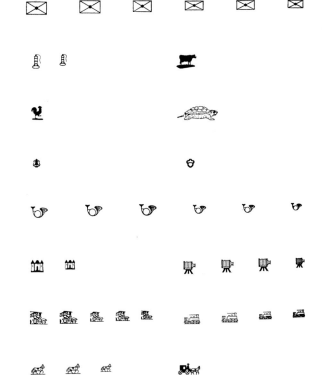

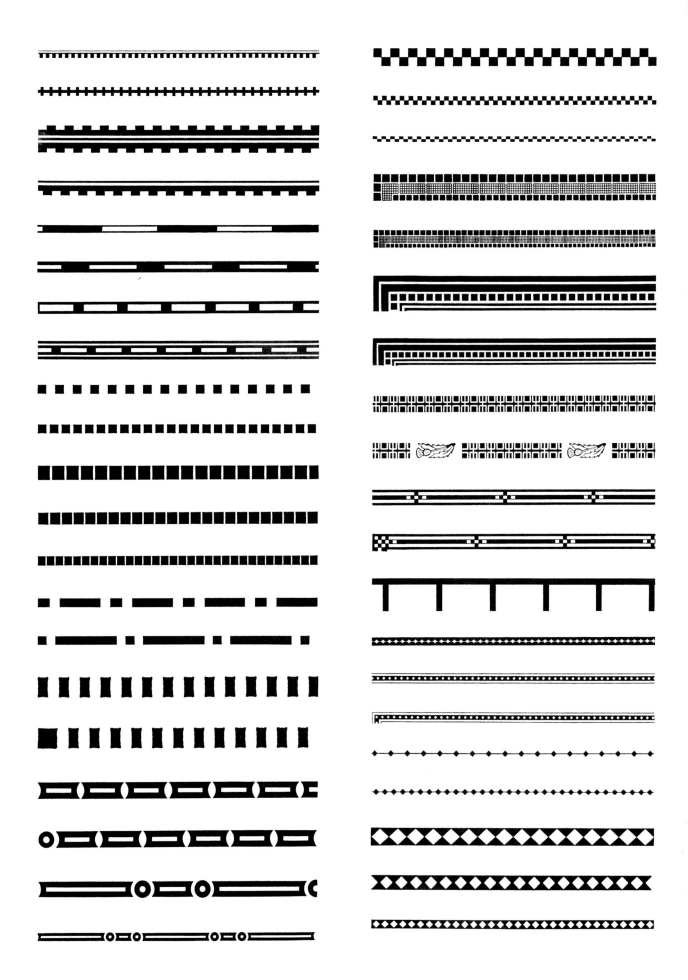

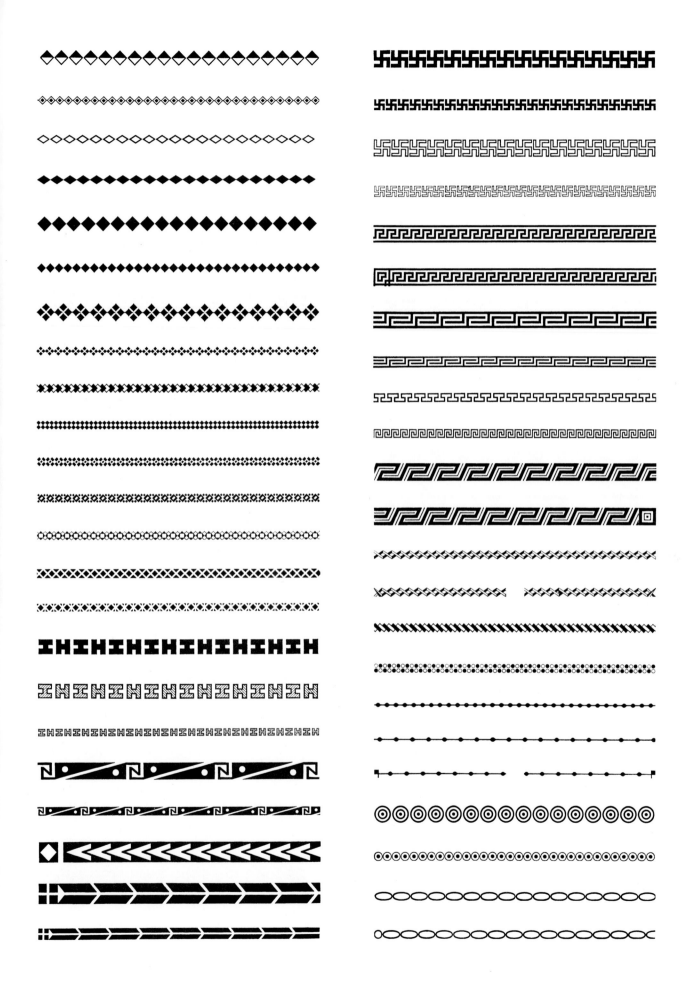

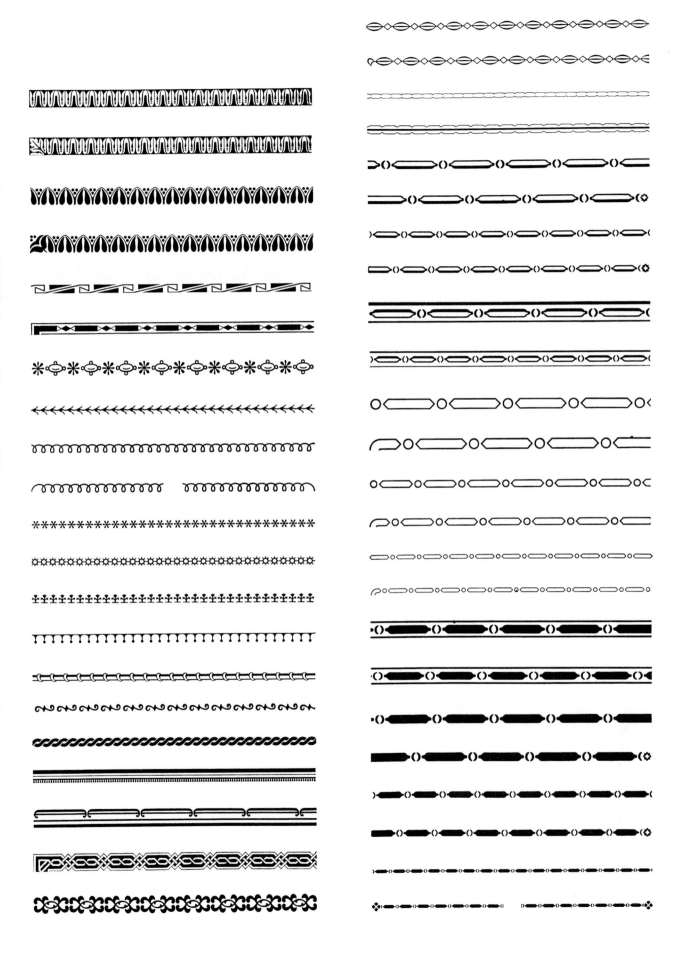

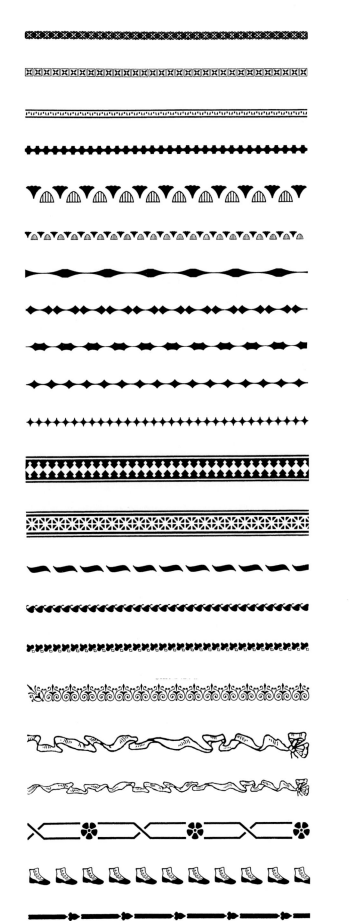
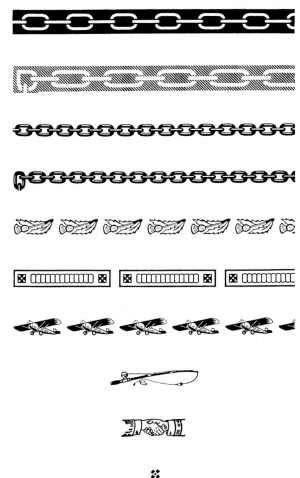

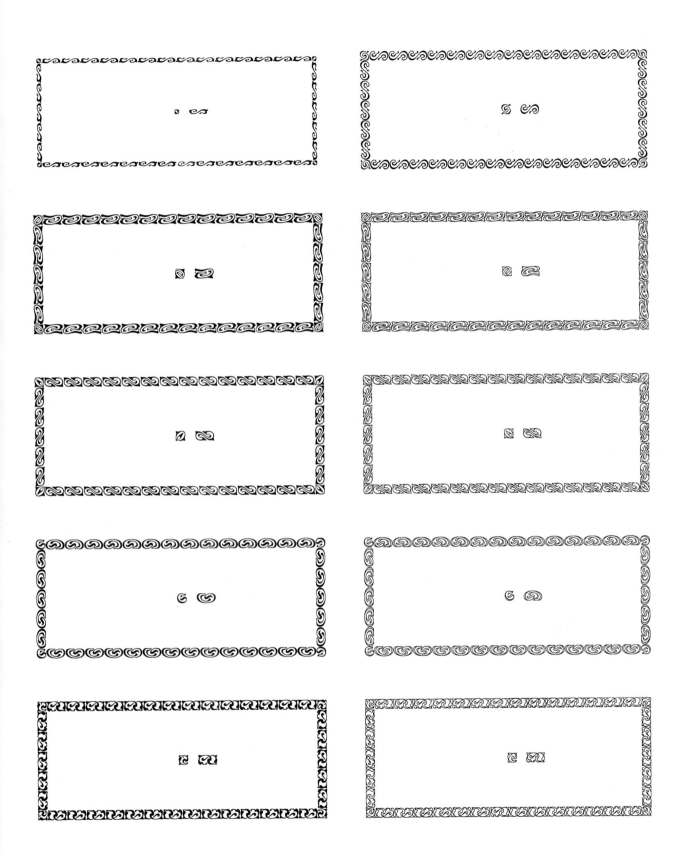

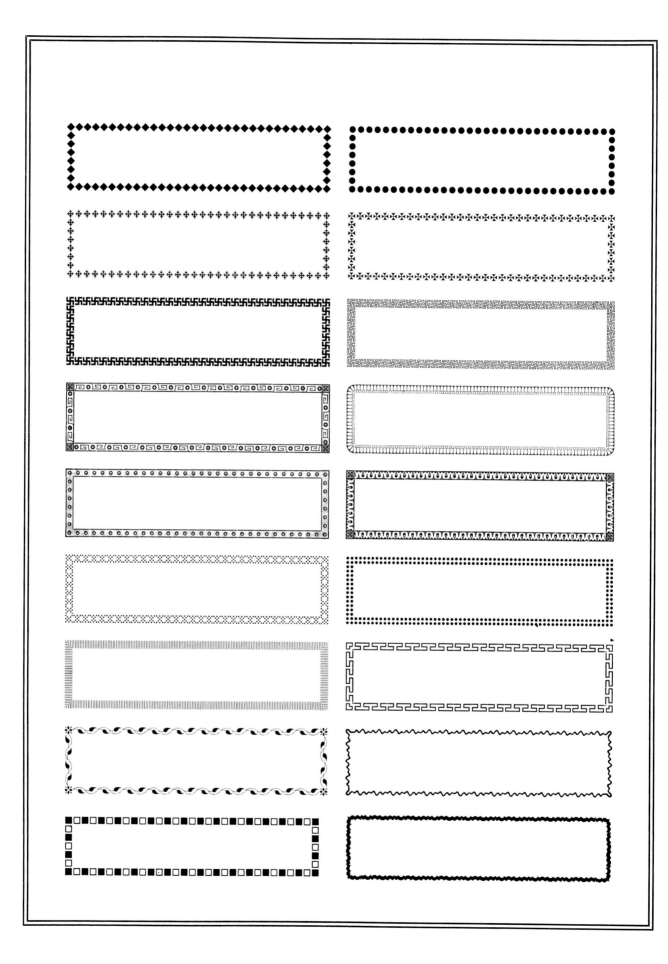

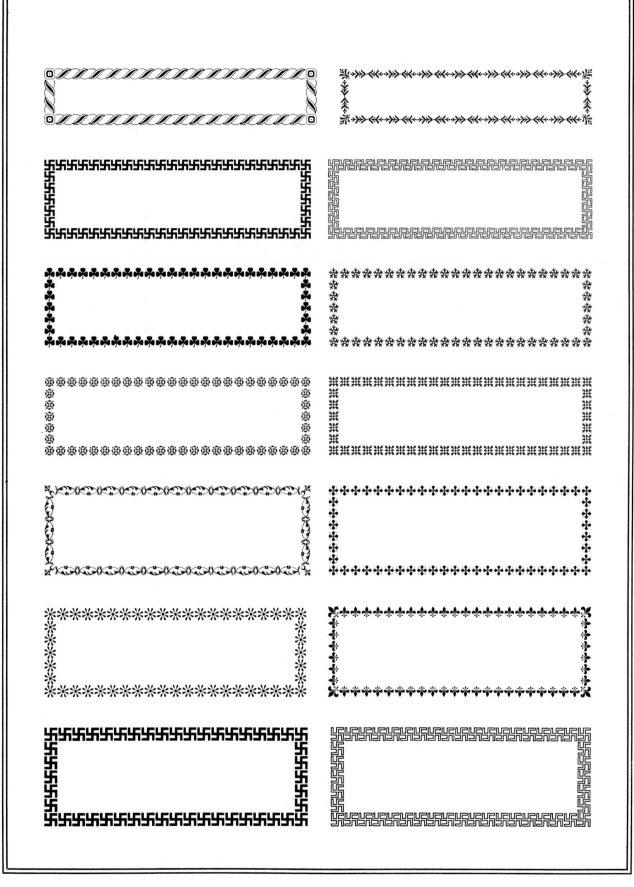

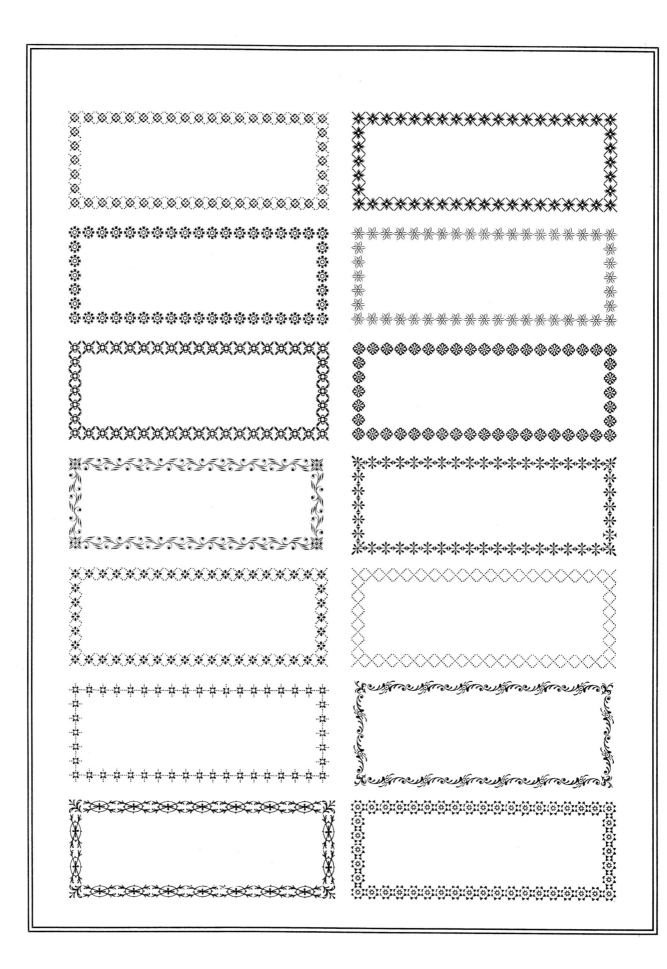

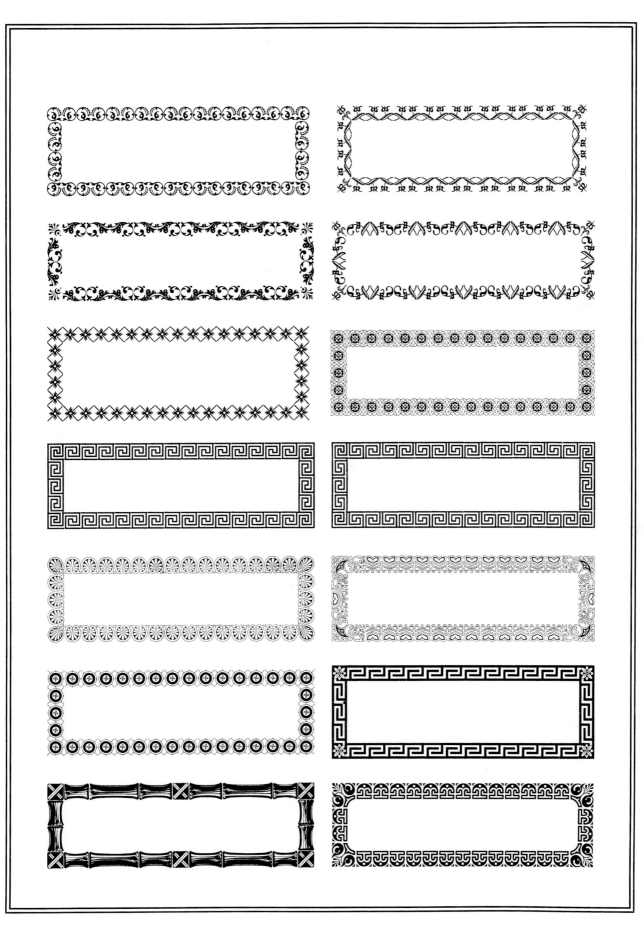

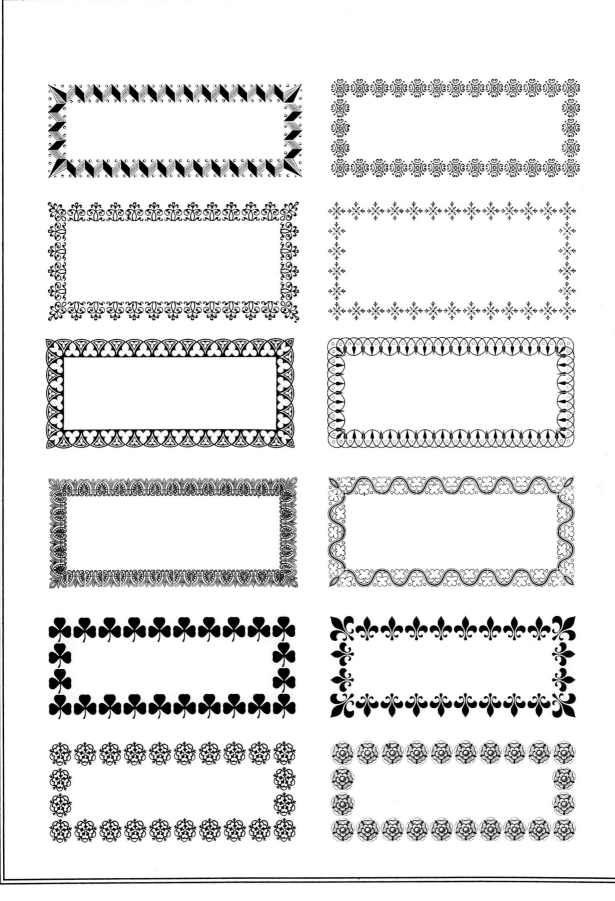

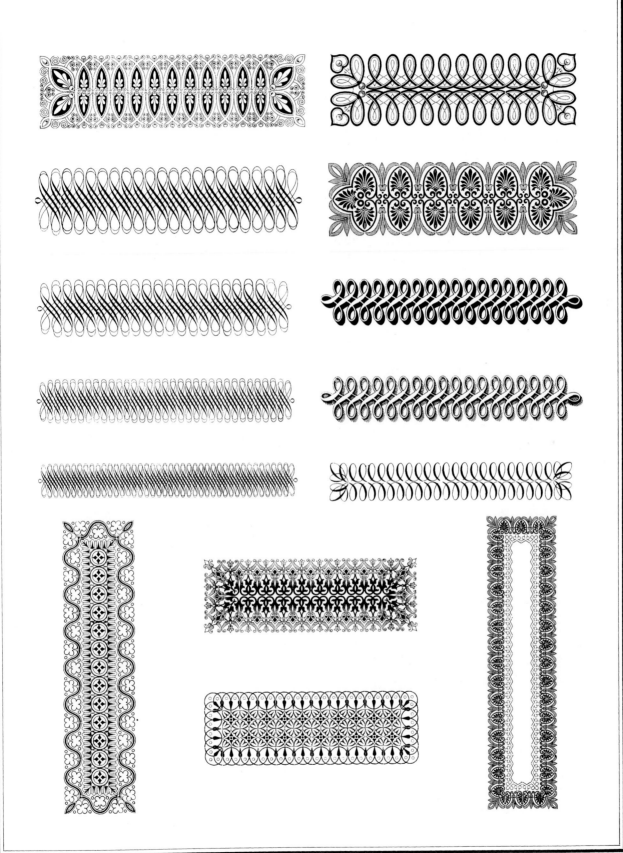

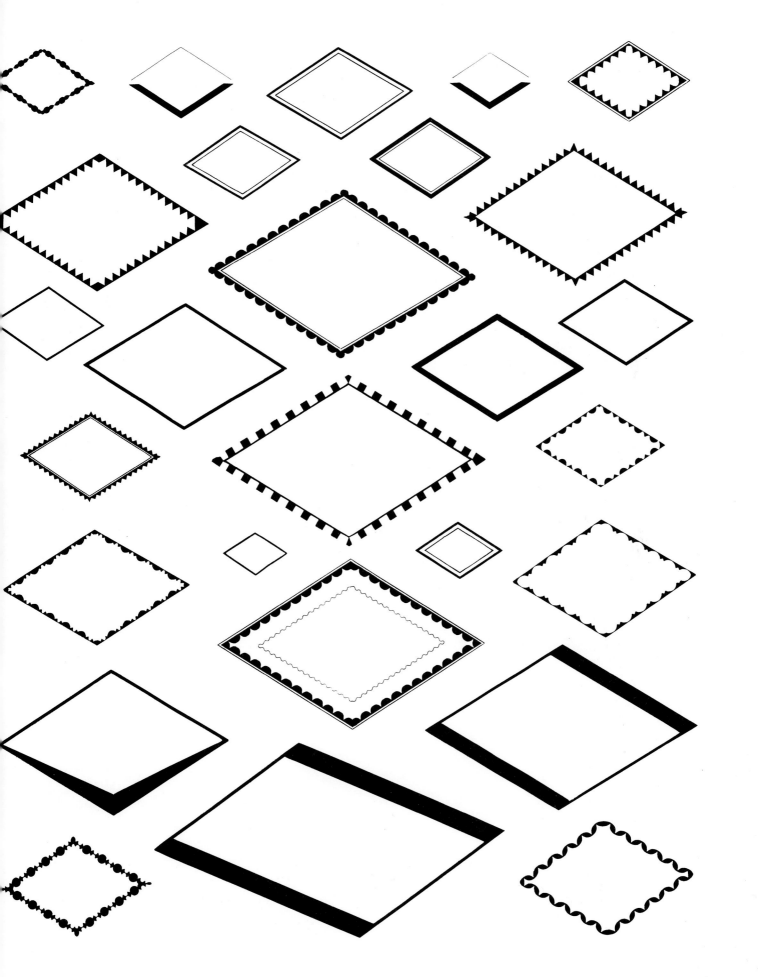

63

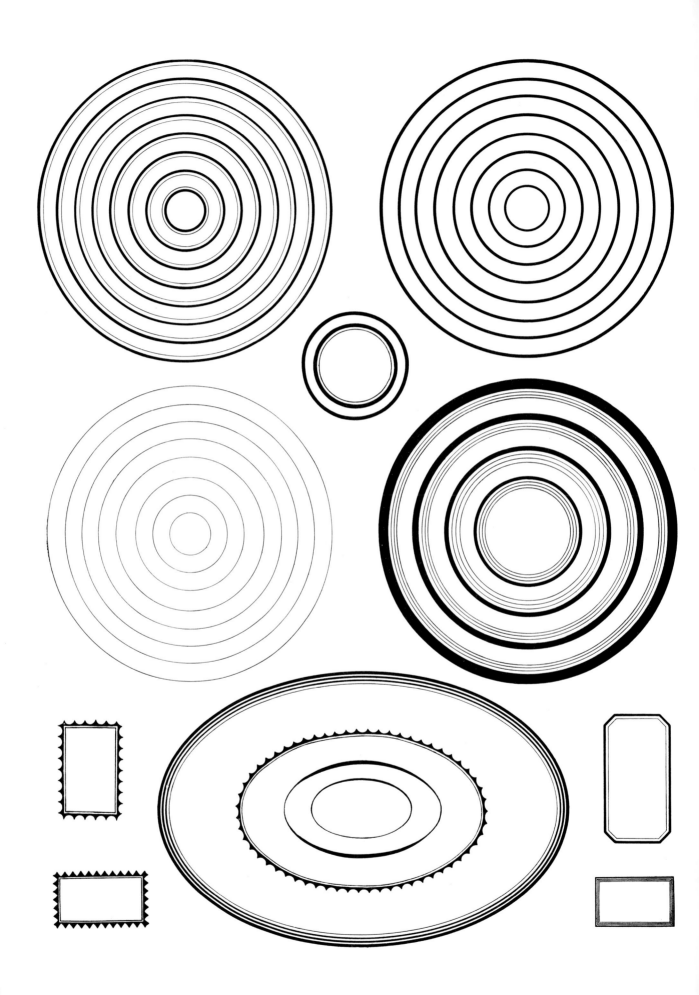

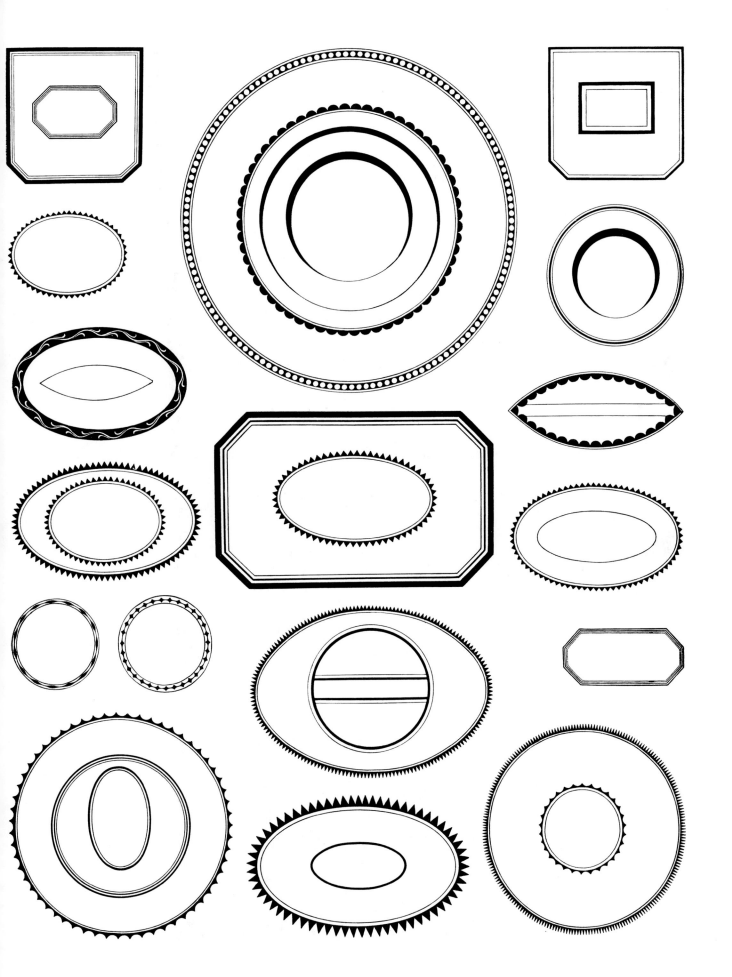

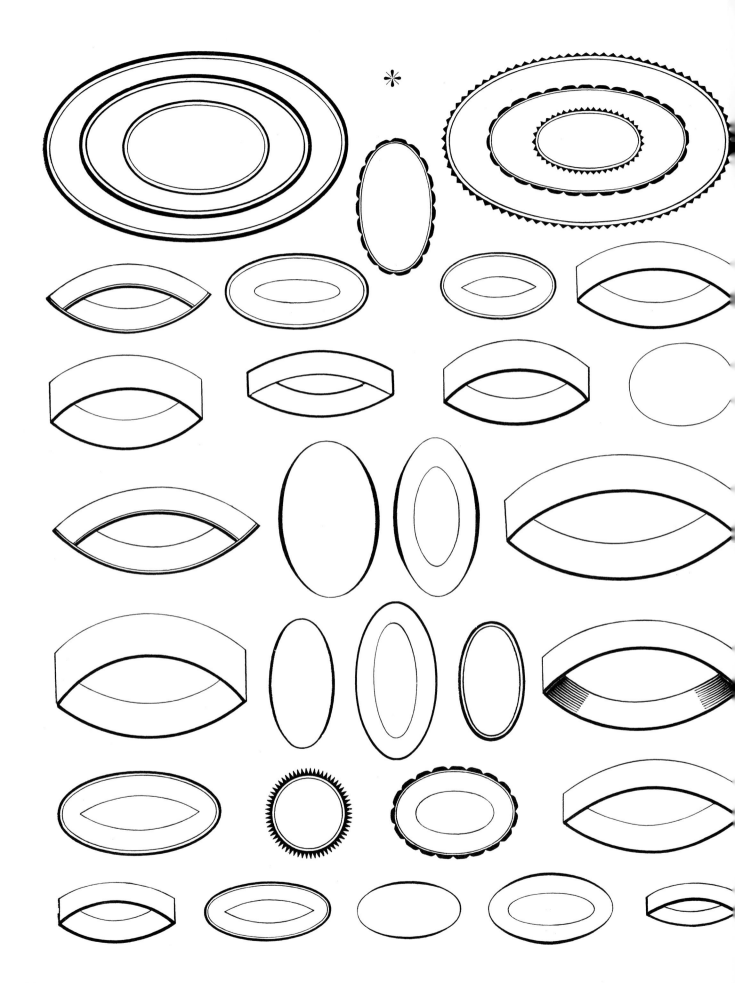

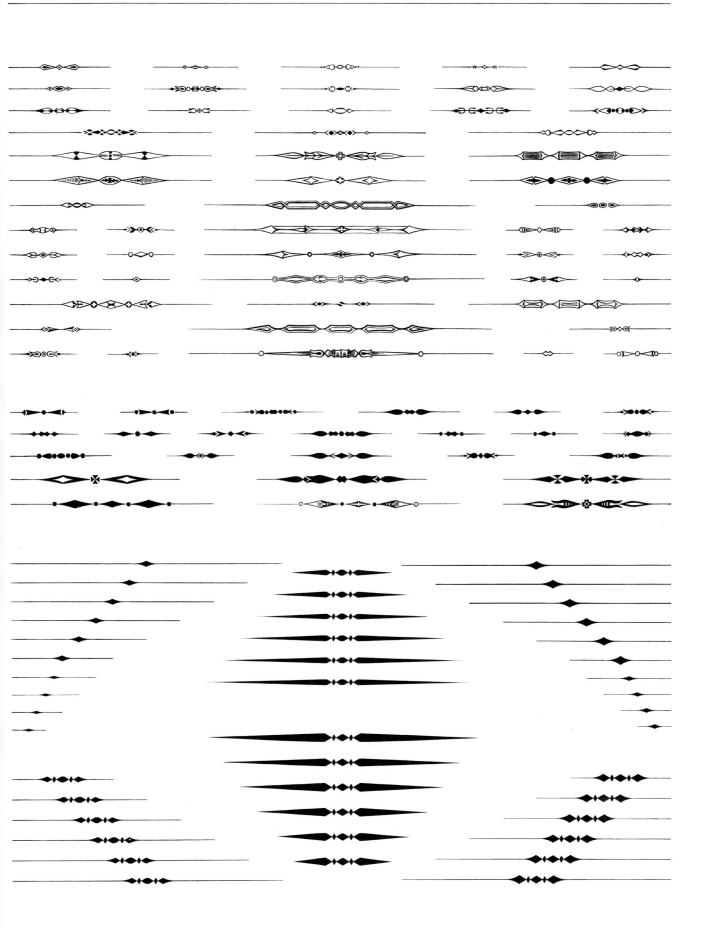

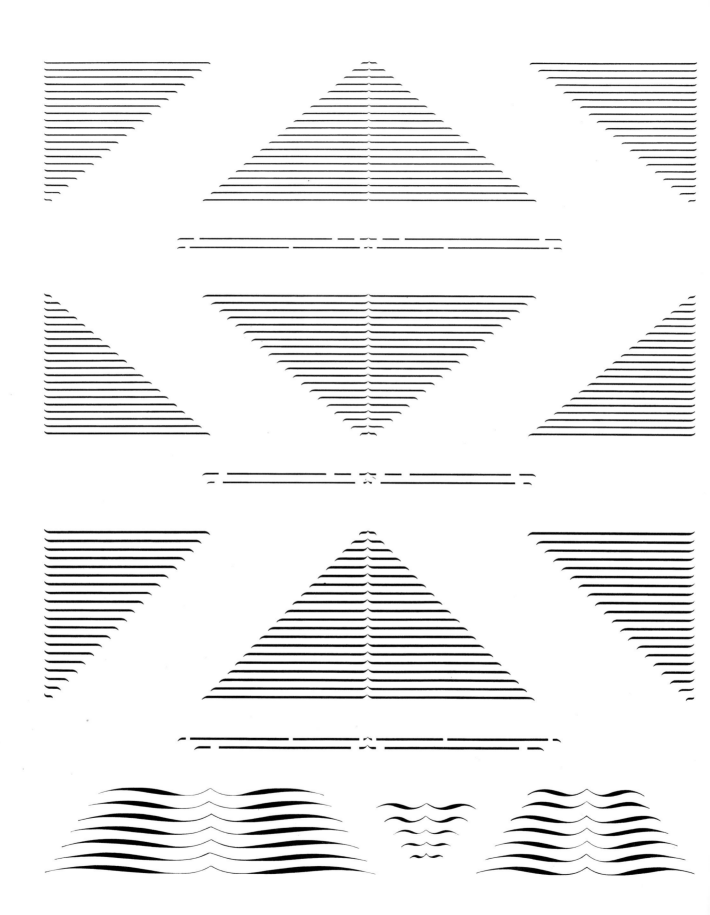

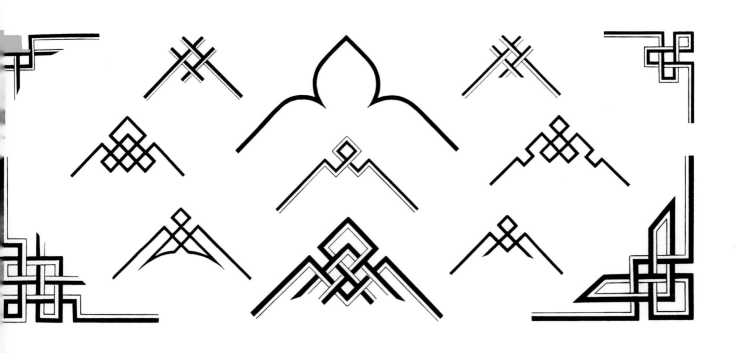

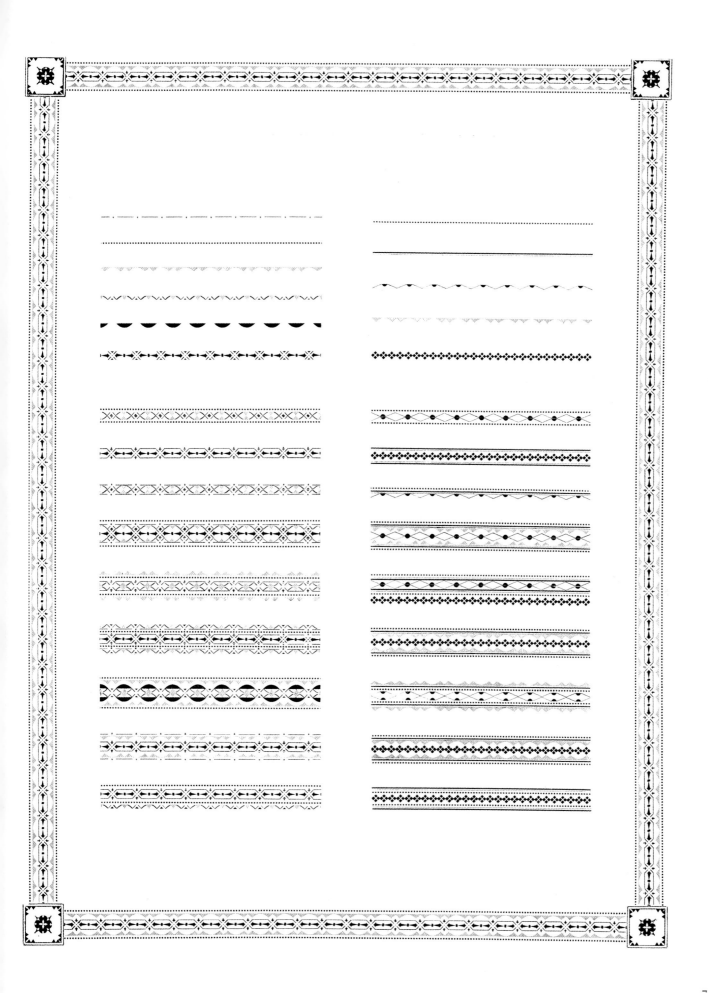

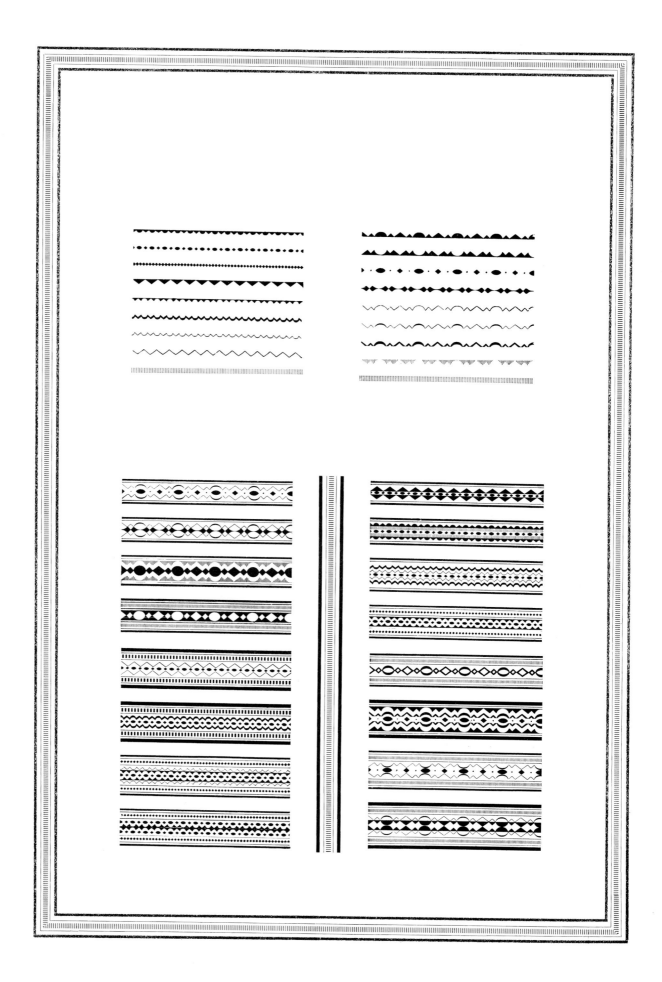

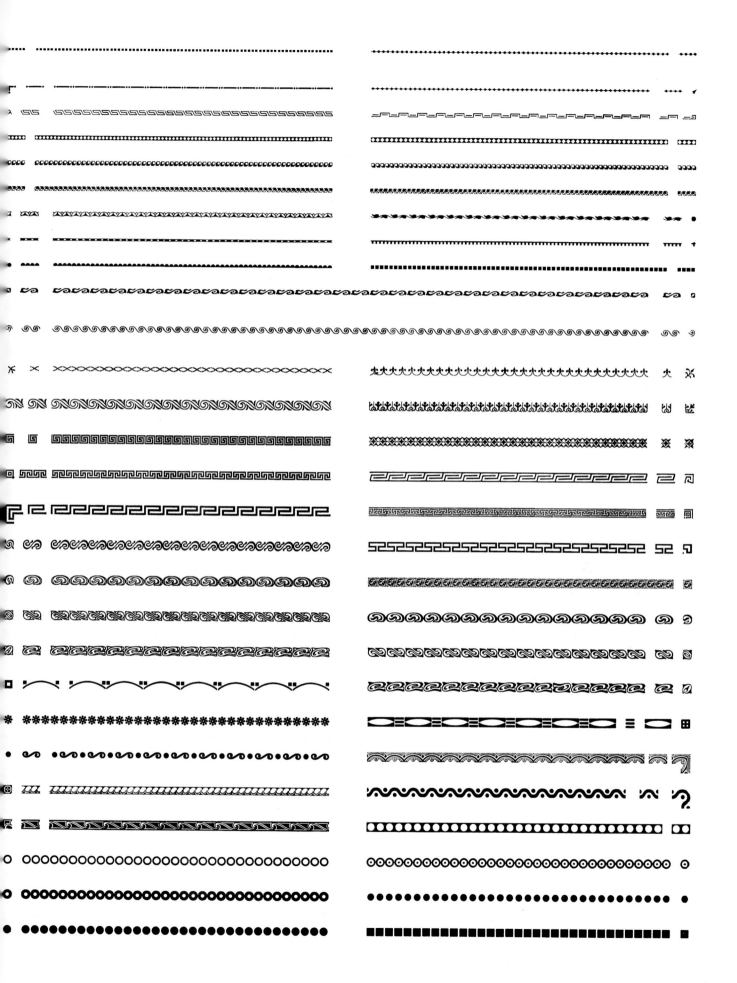

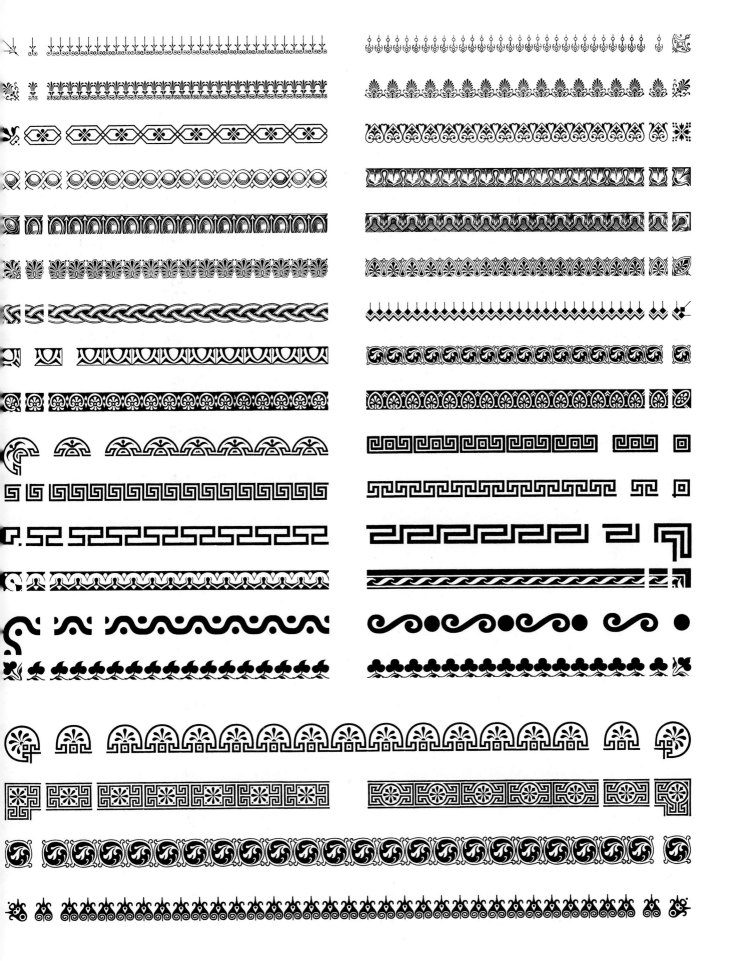

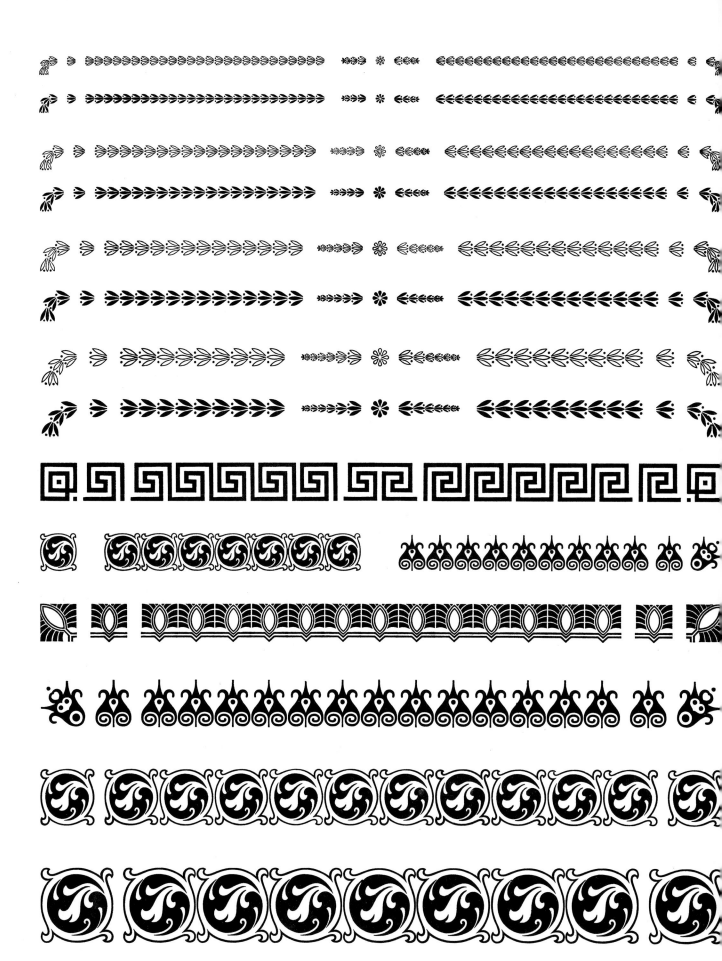

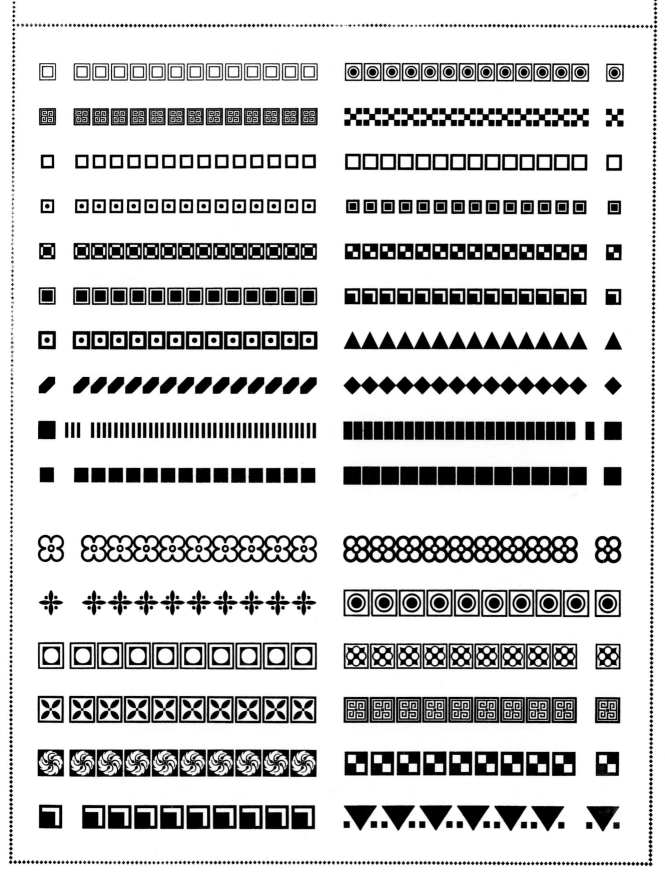

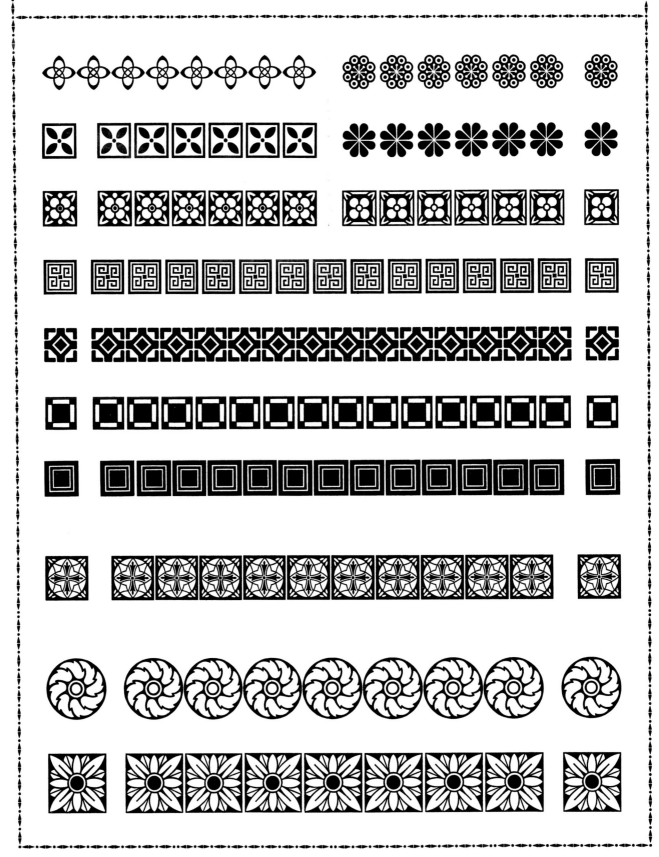

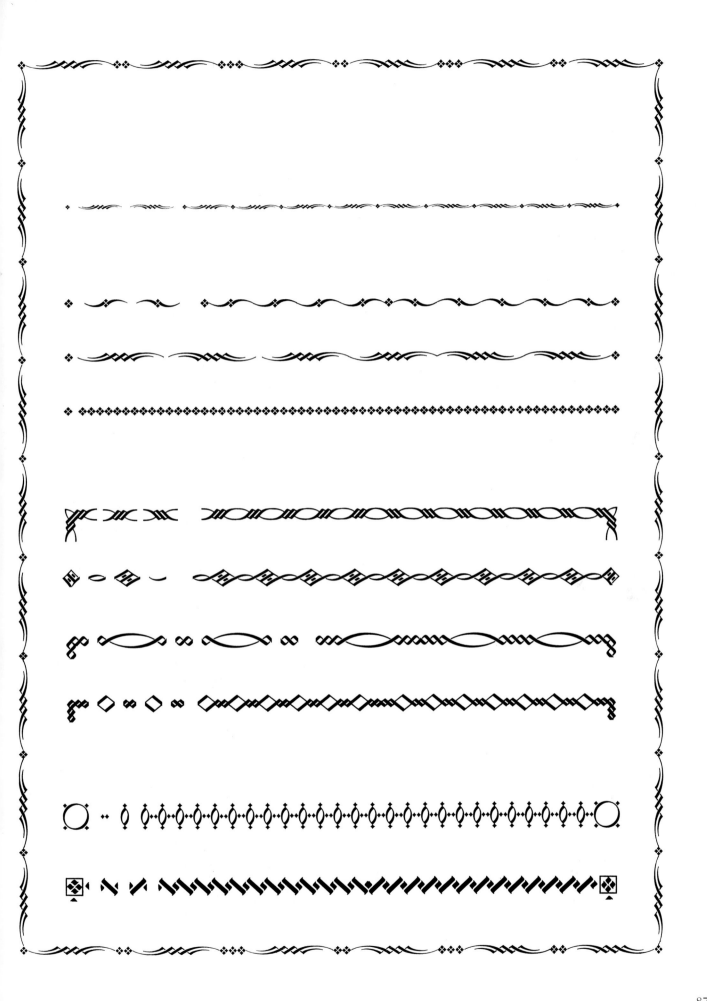

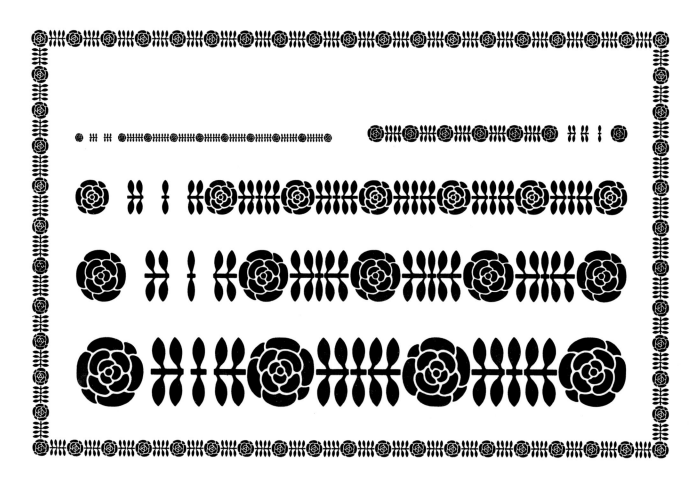

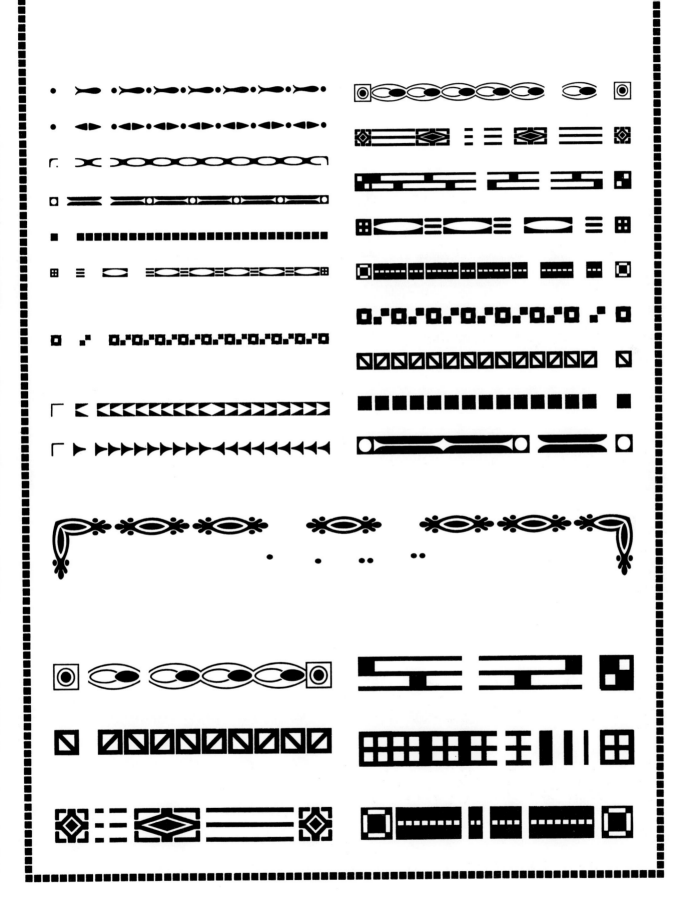

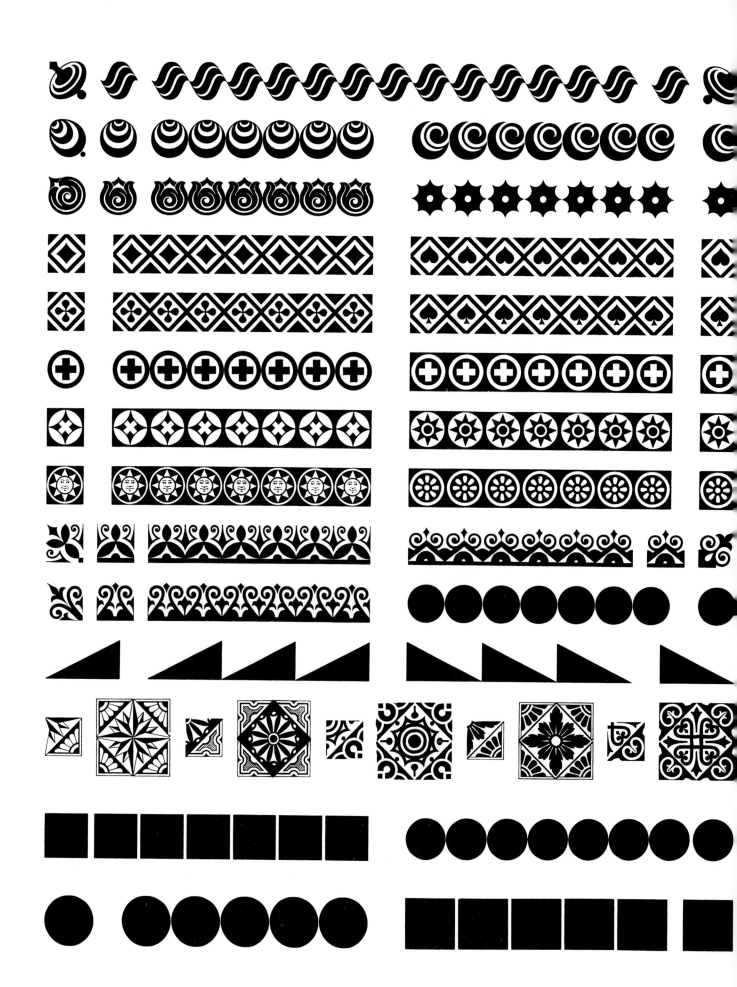

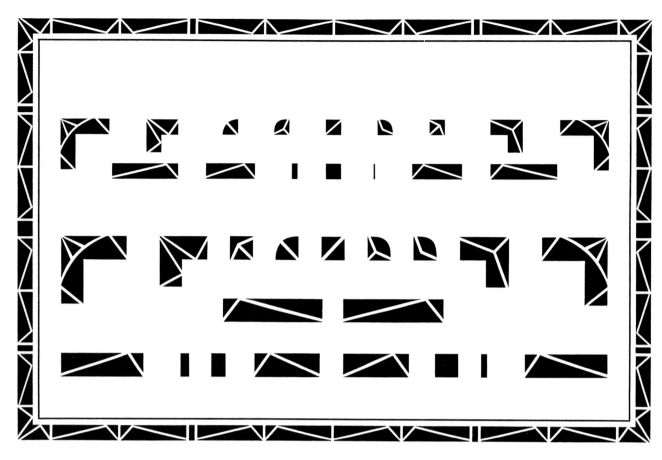

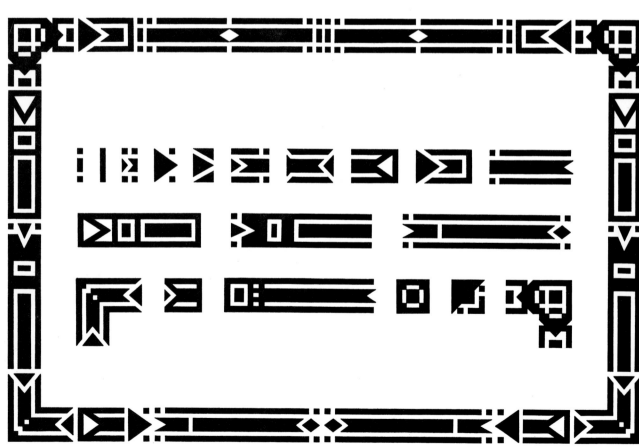

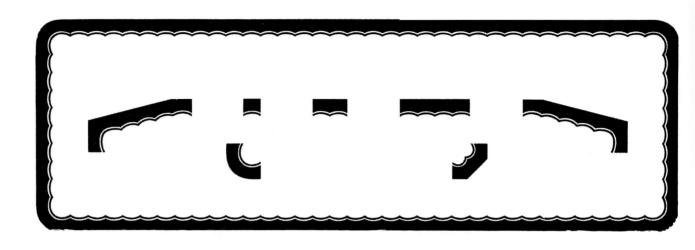

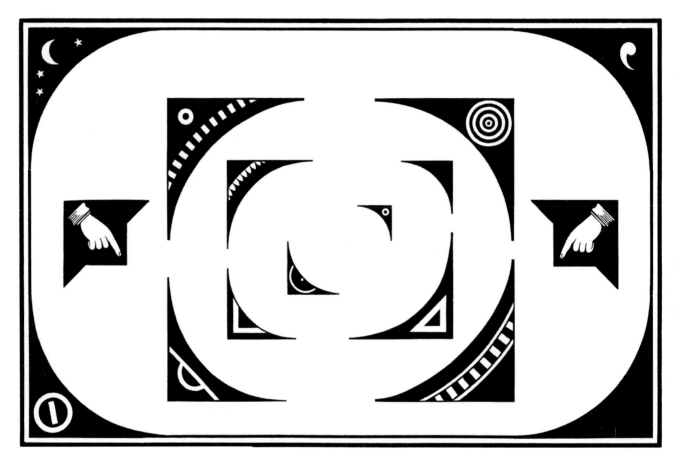

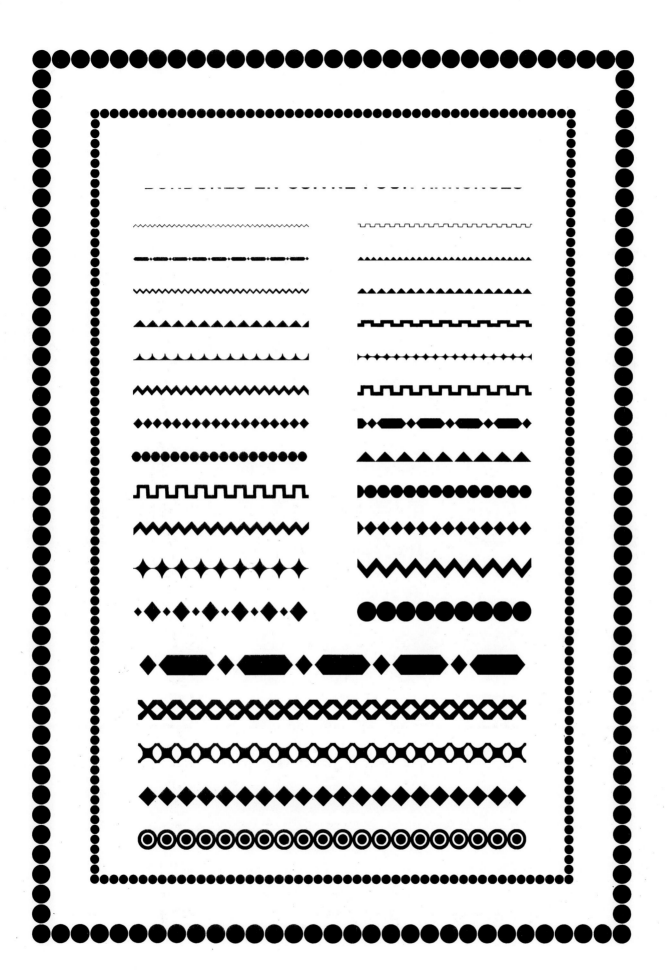

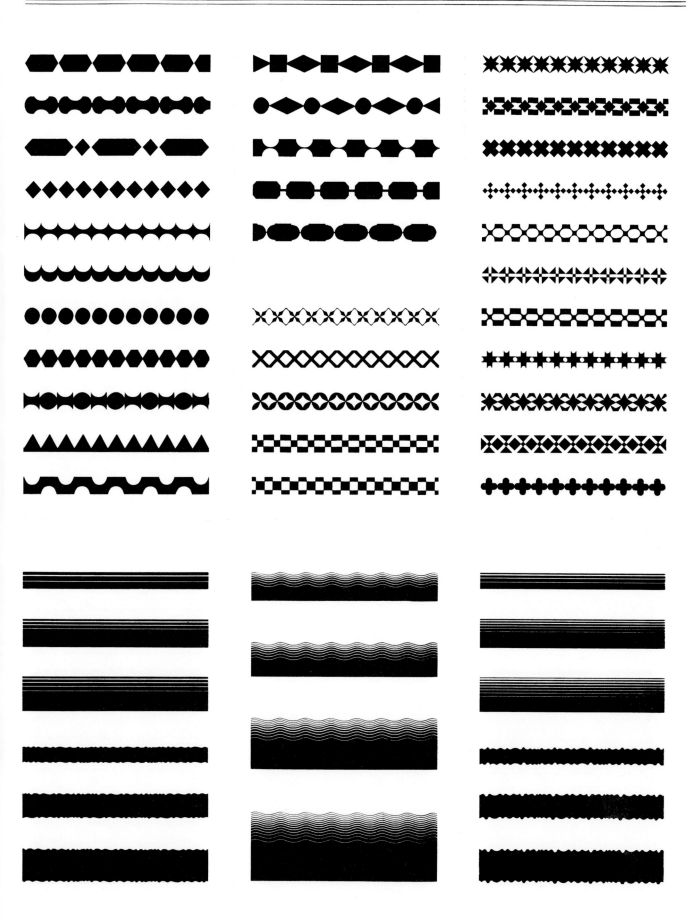

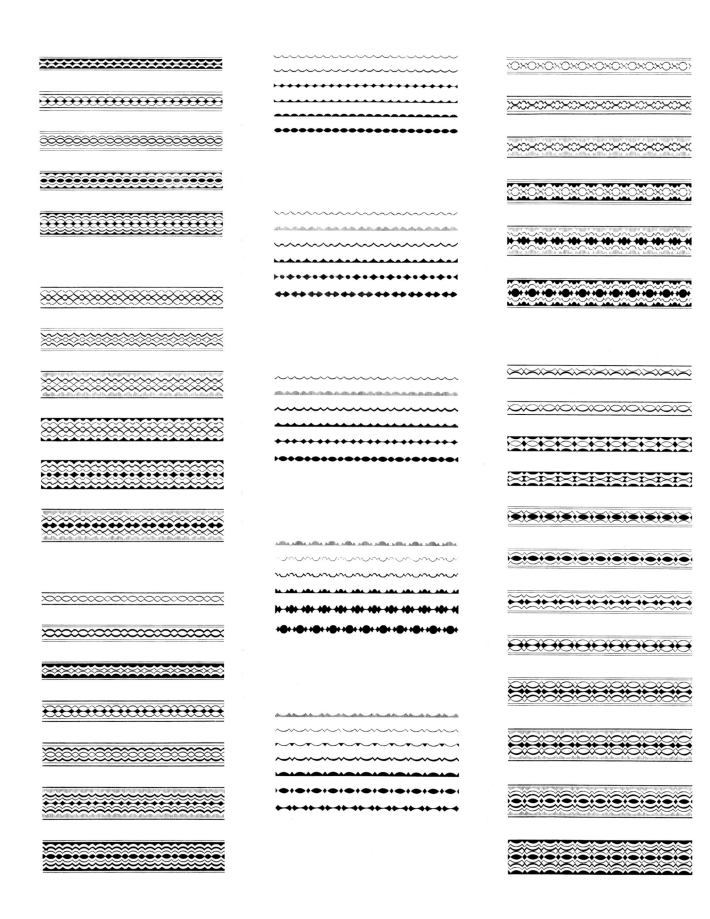

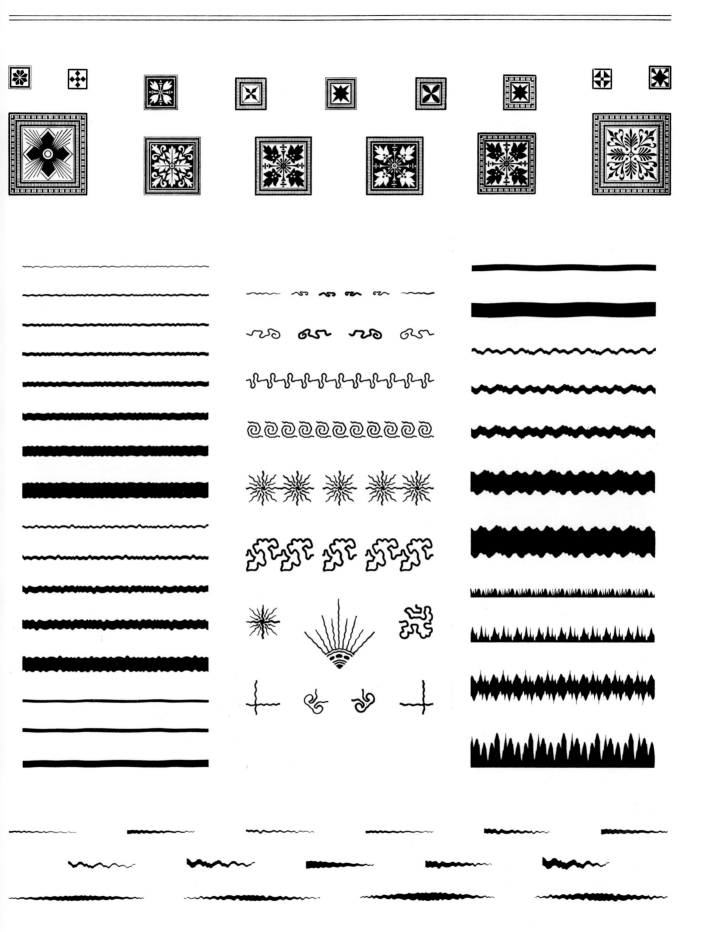

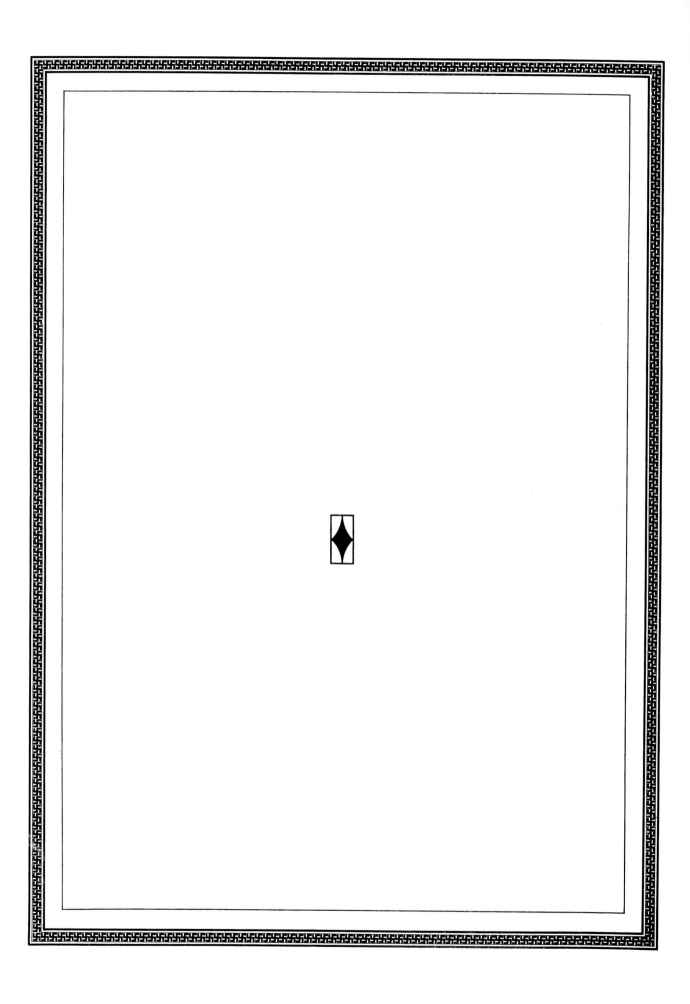

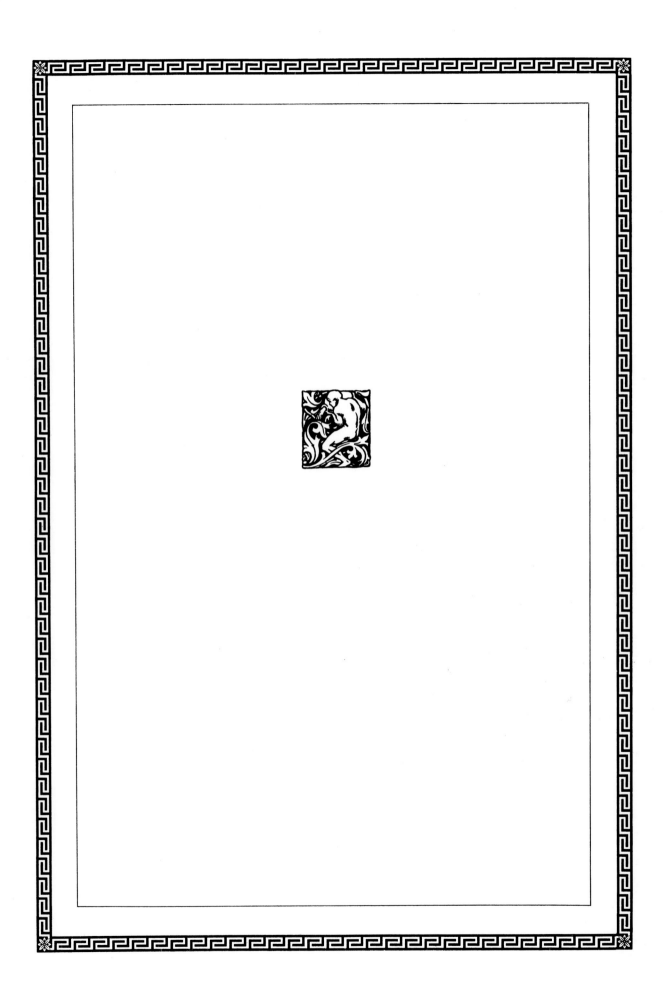

106

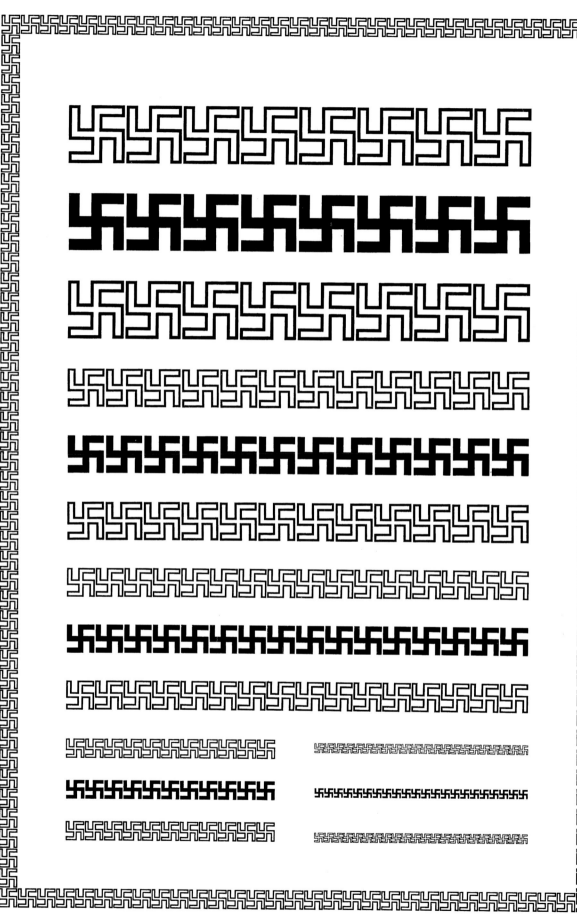

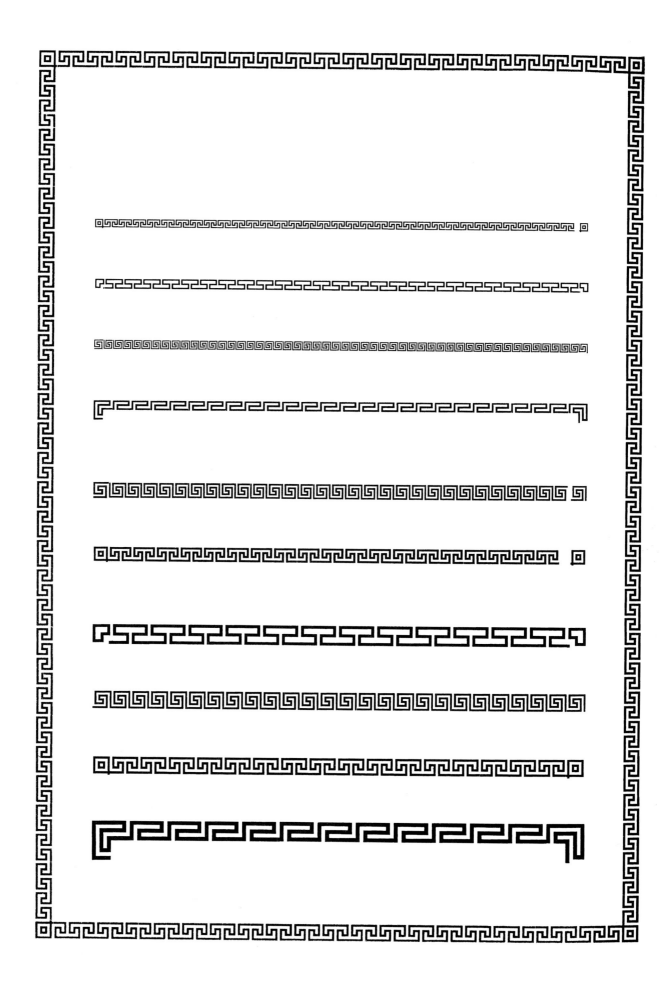

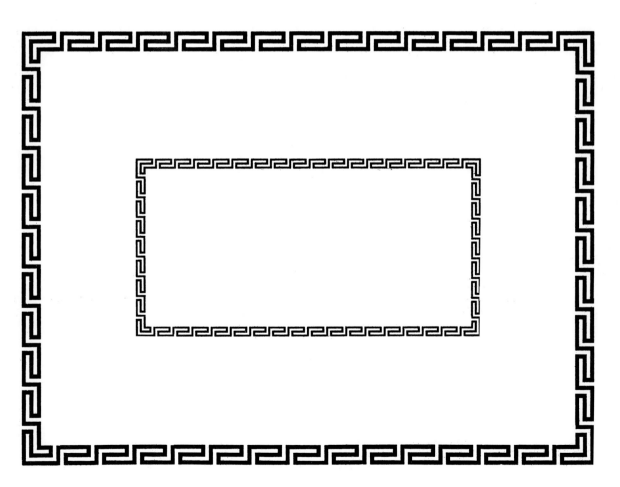

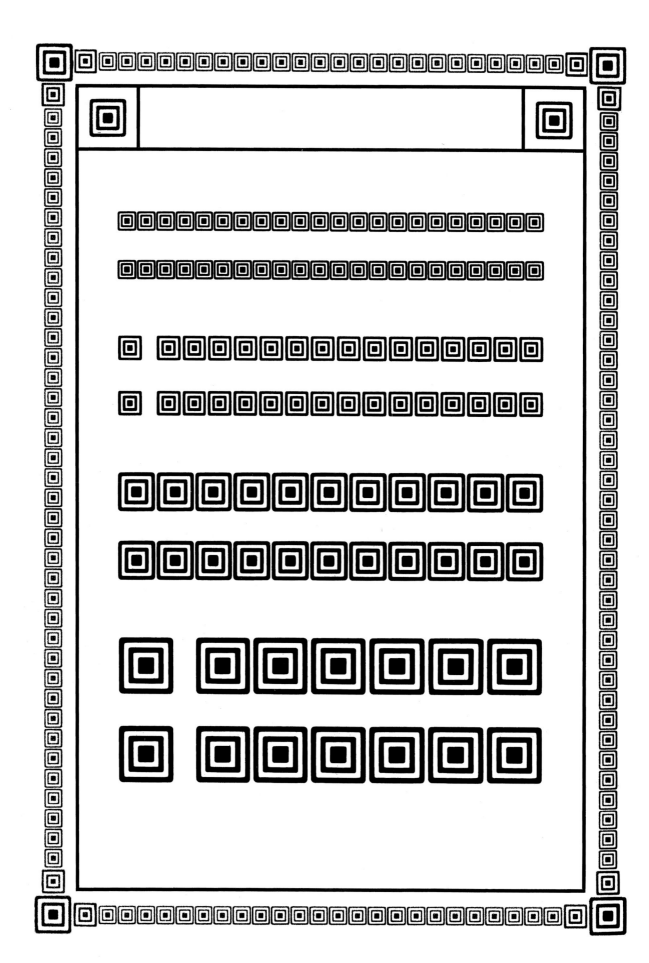

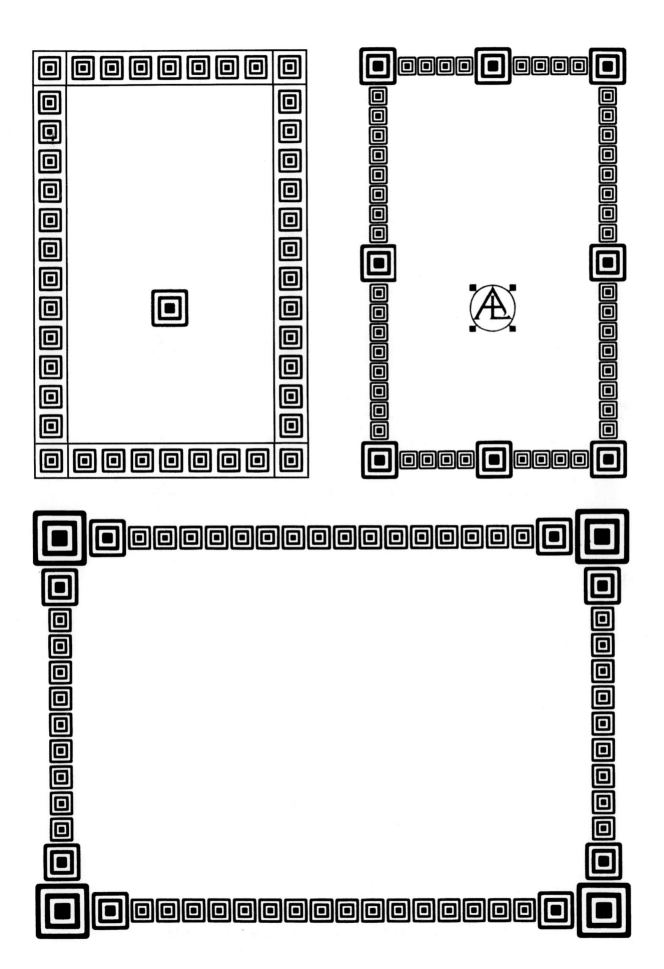

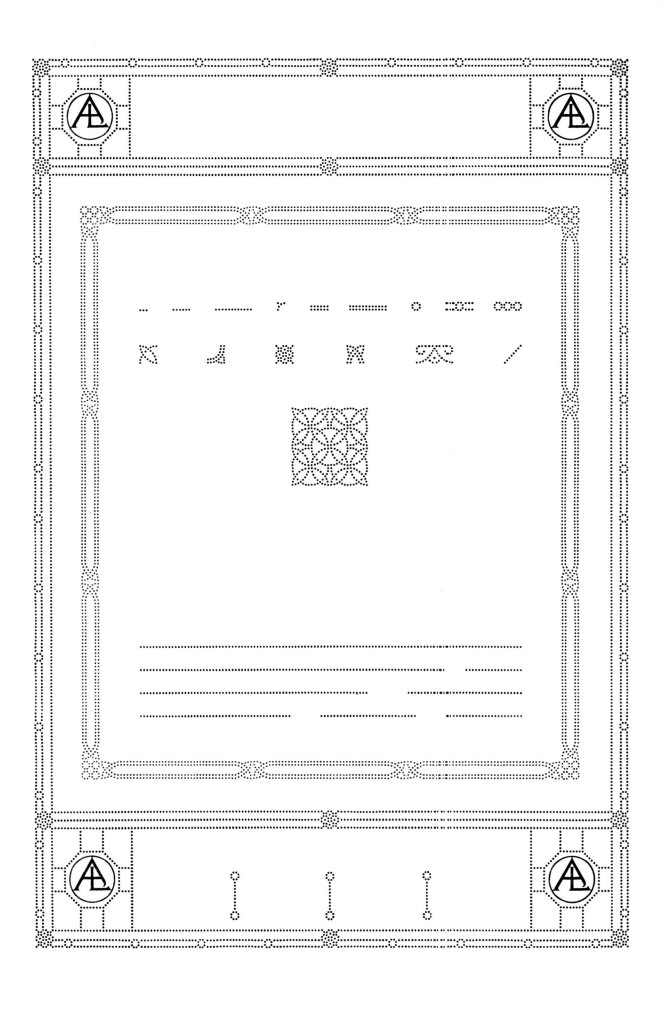

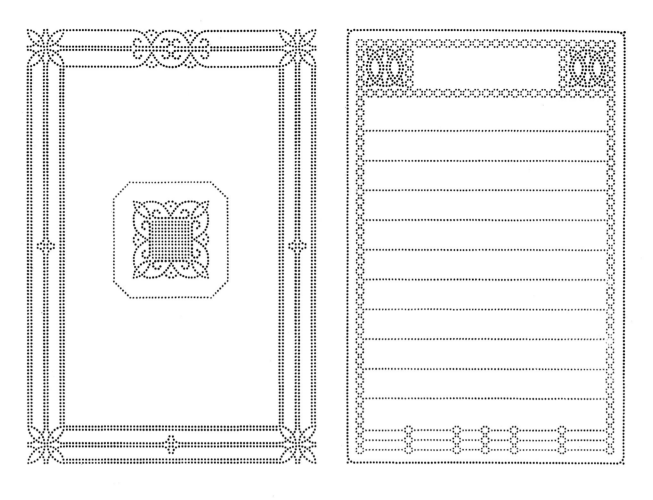

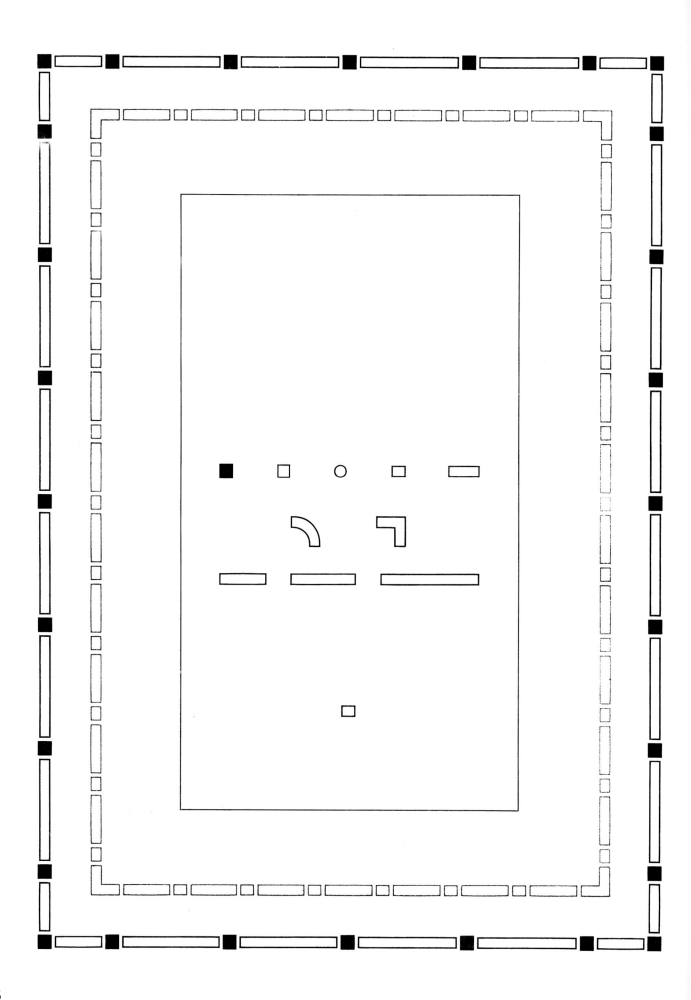

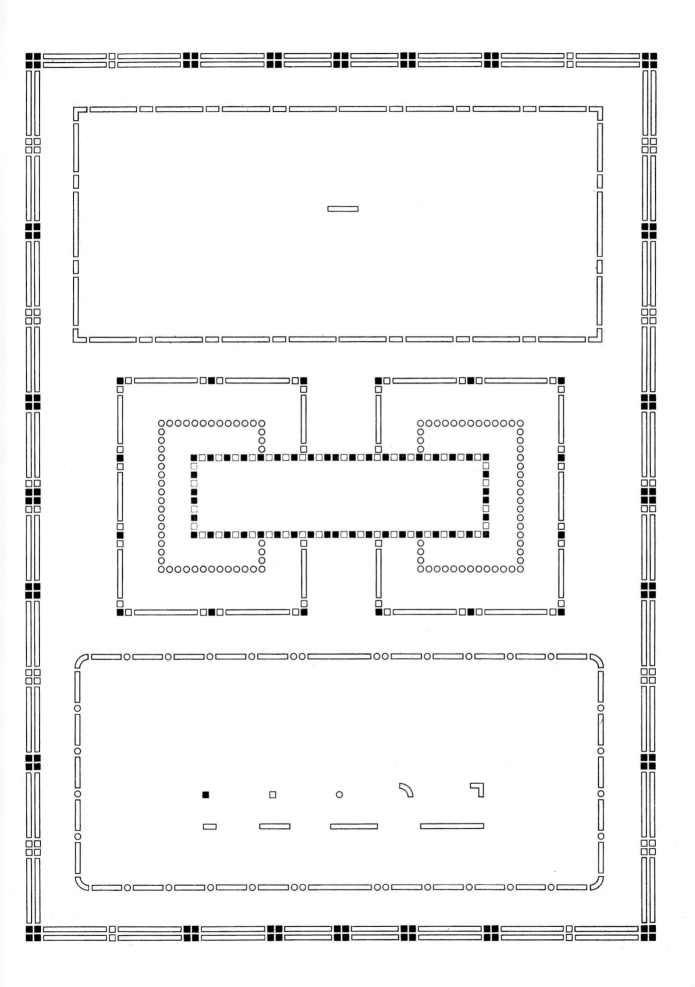

117

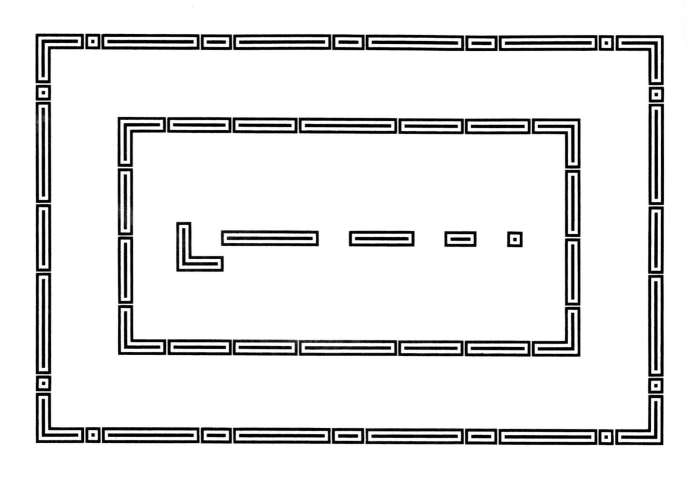

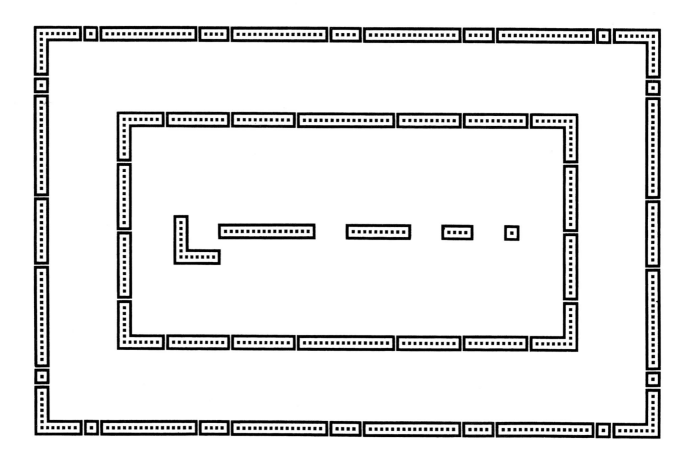

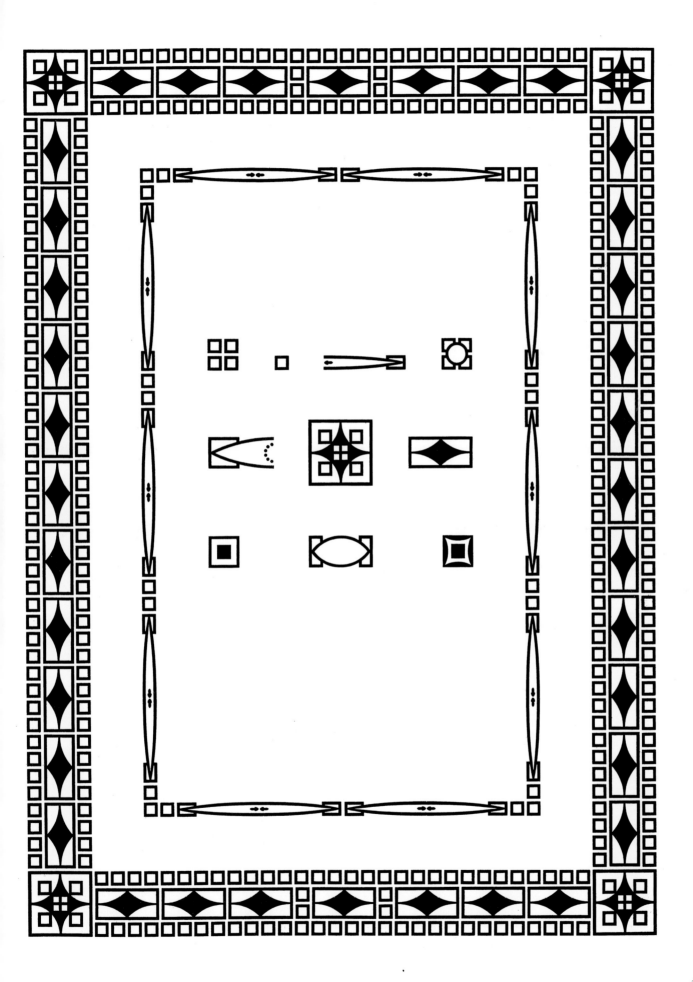

119

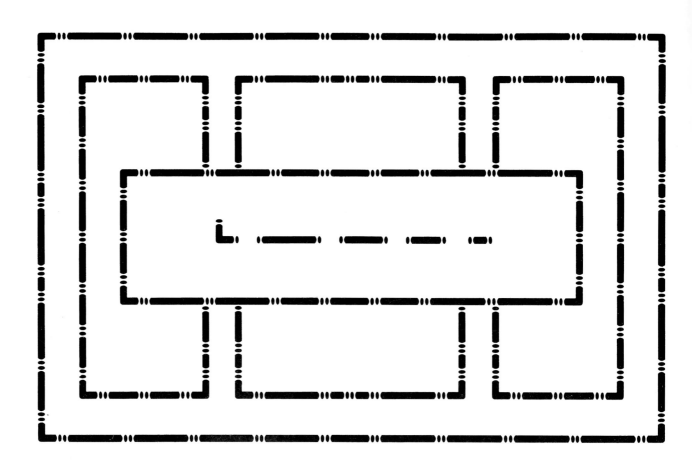

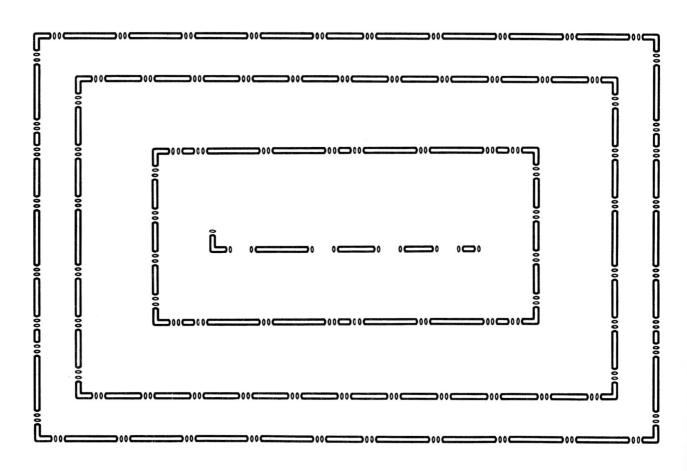

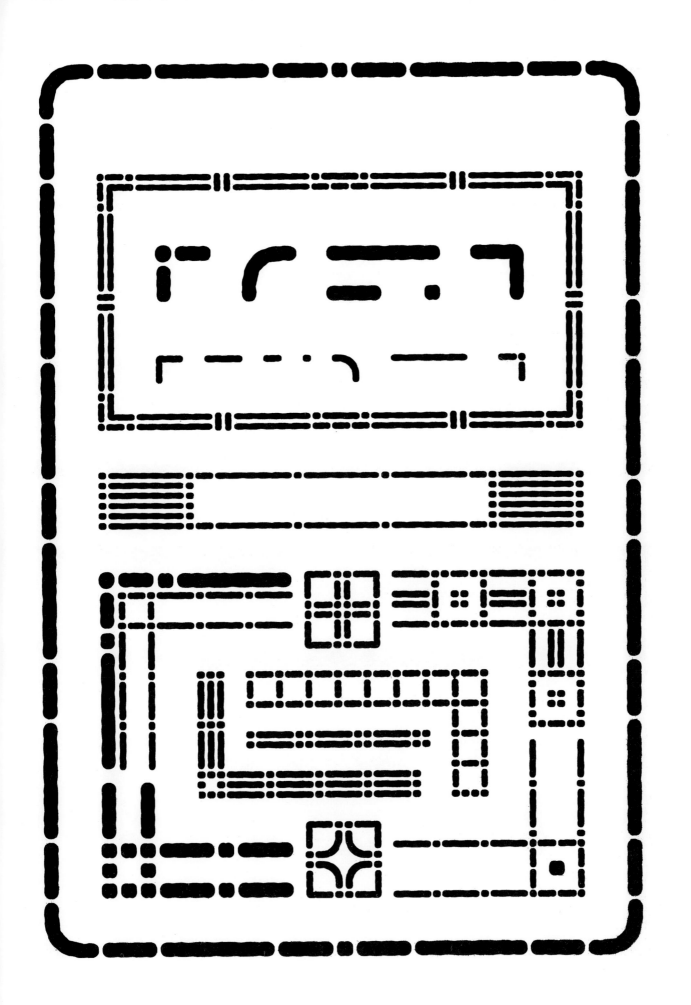

121

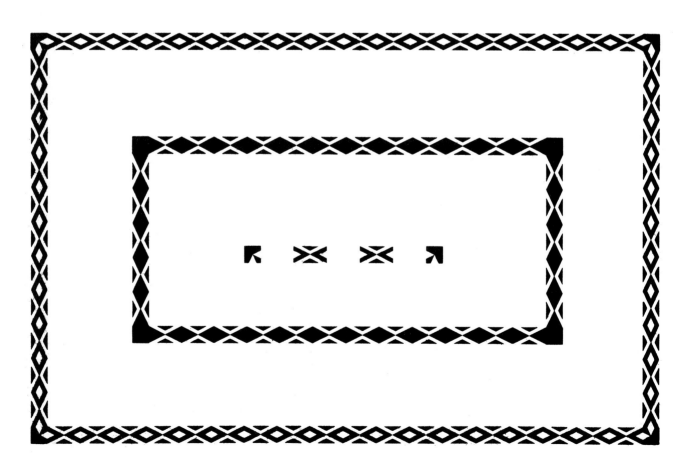

123

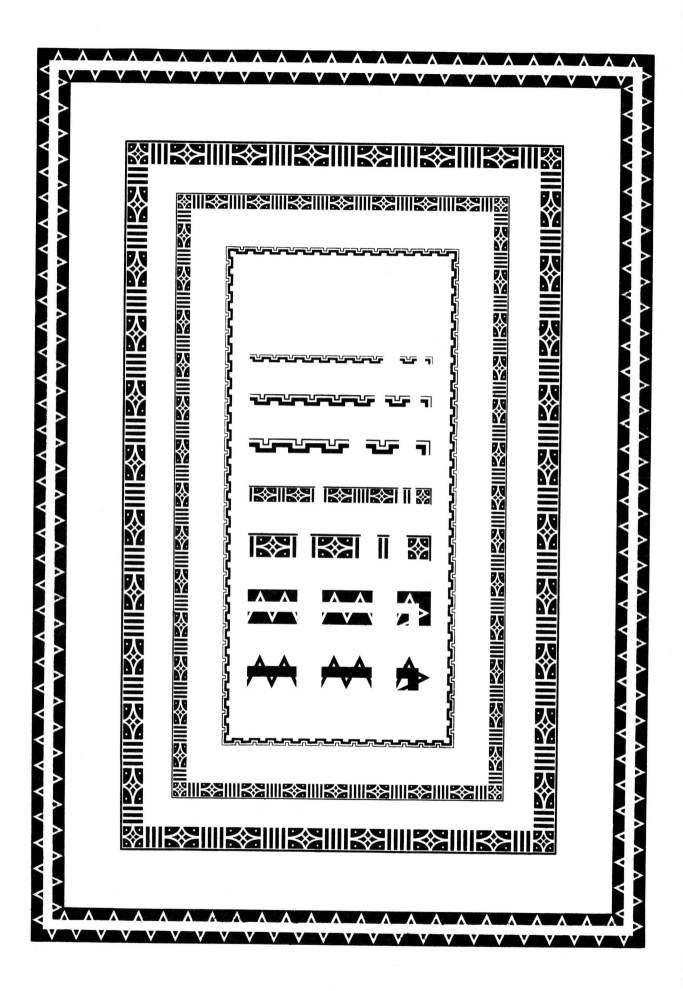

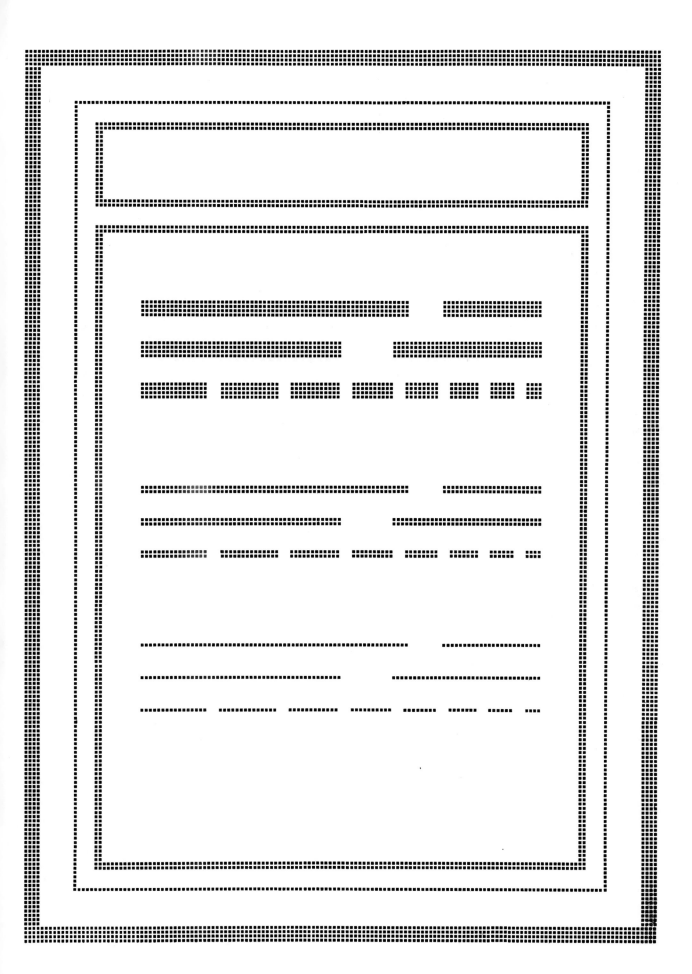

127

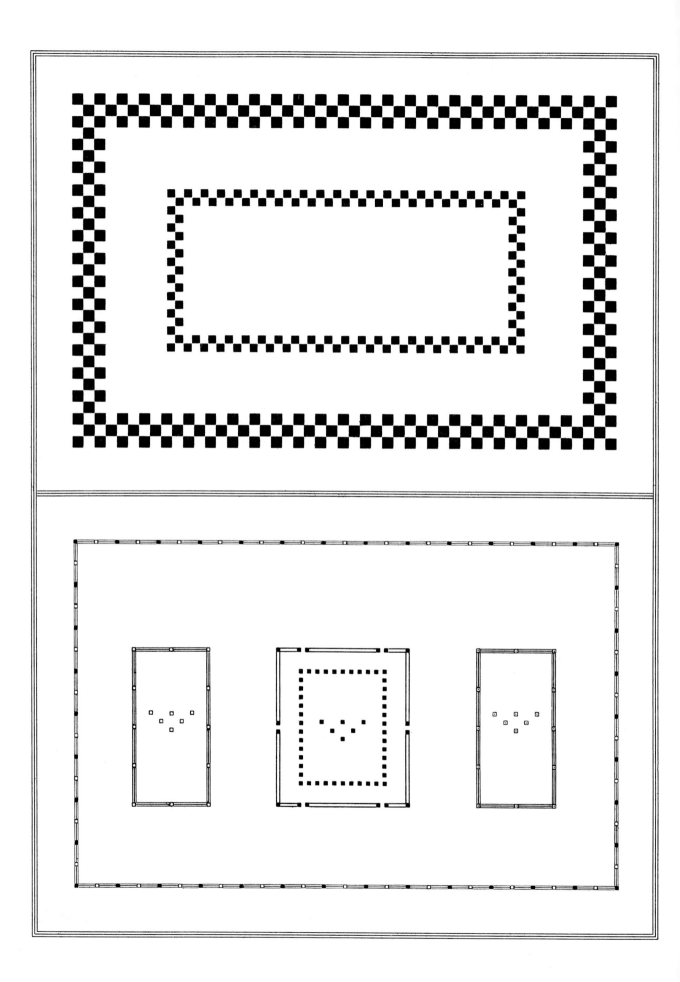

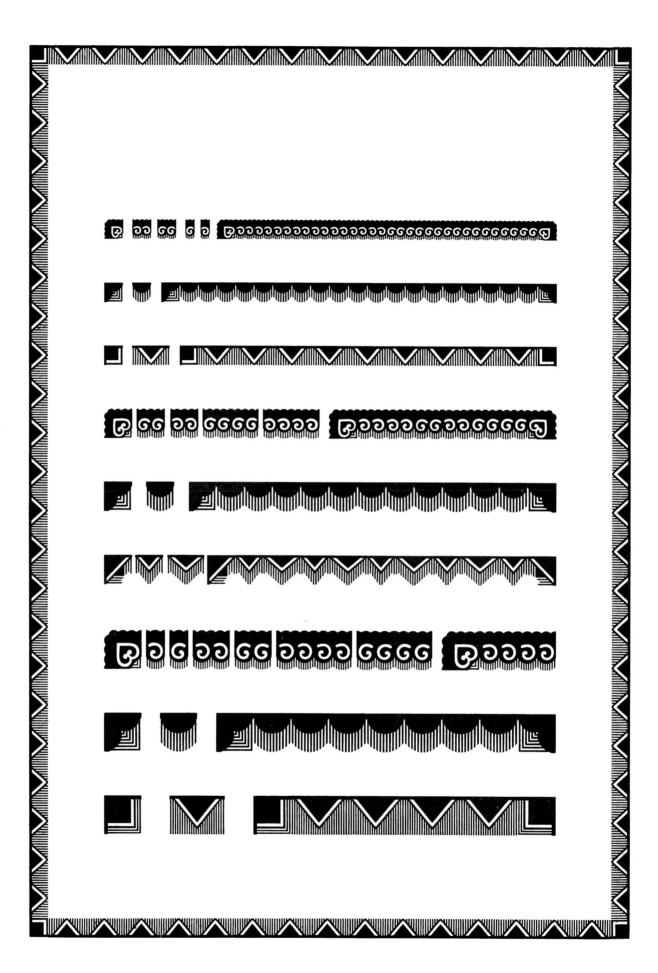

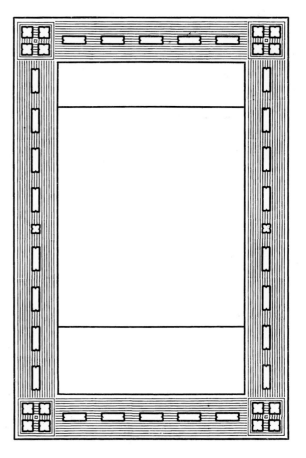

134

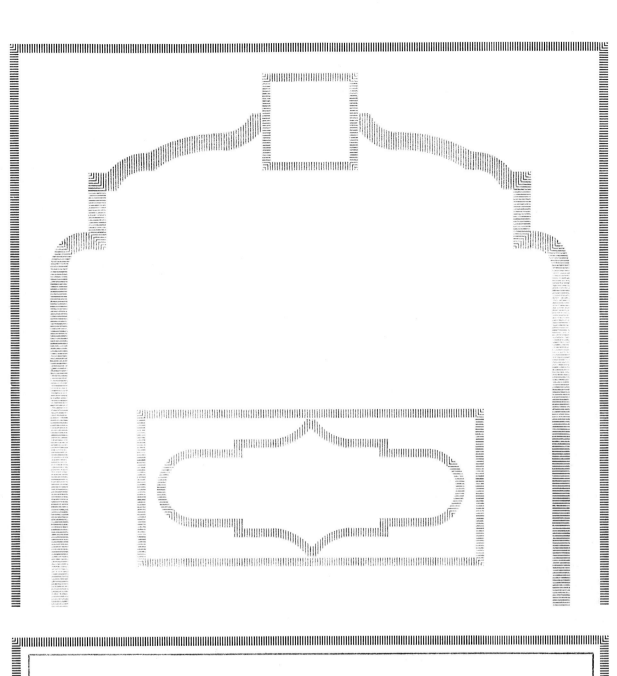

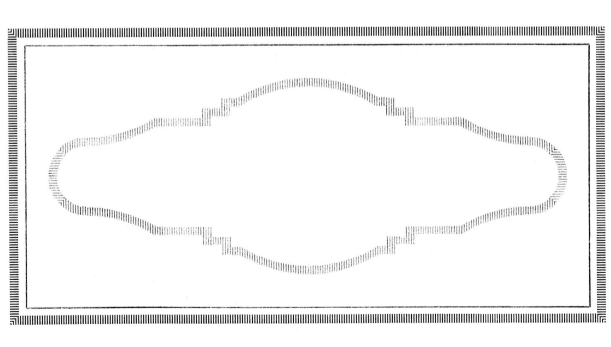

135

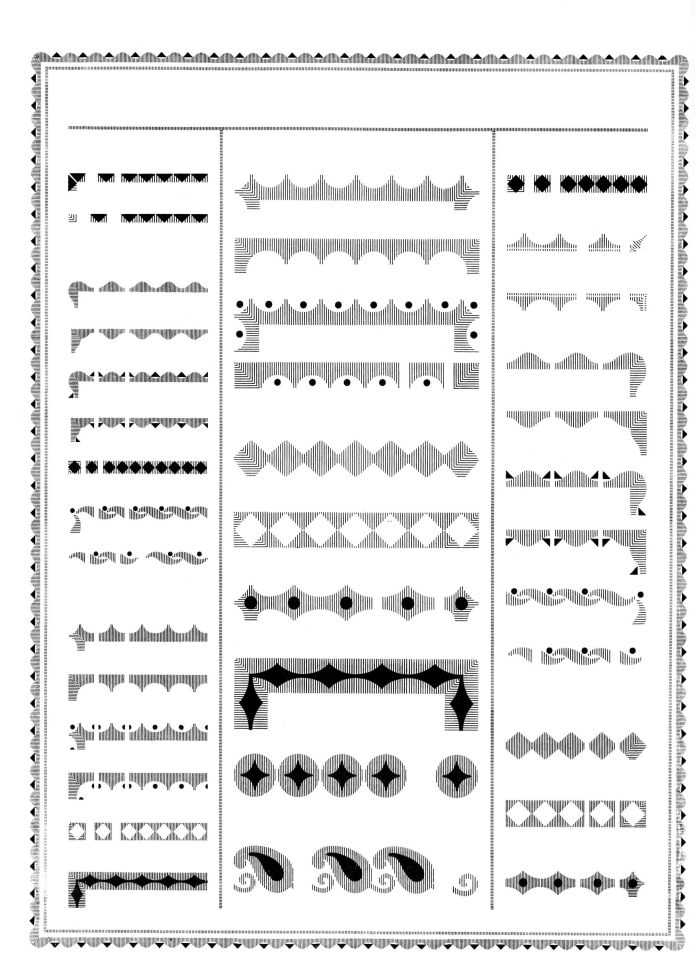

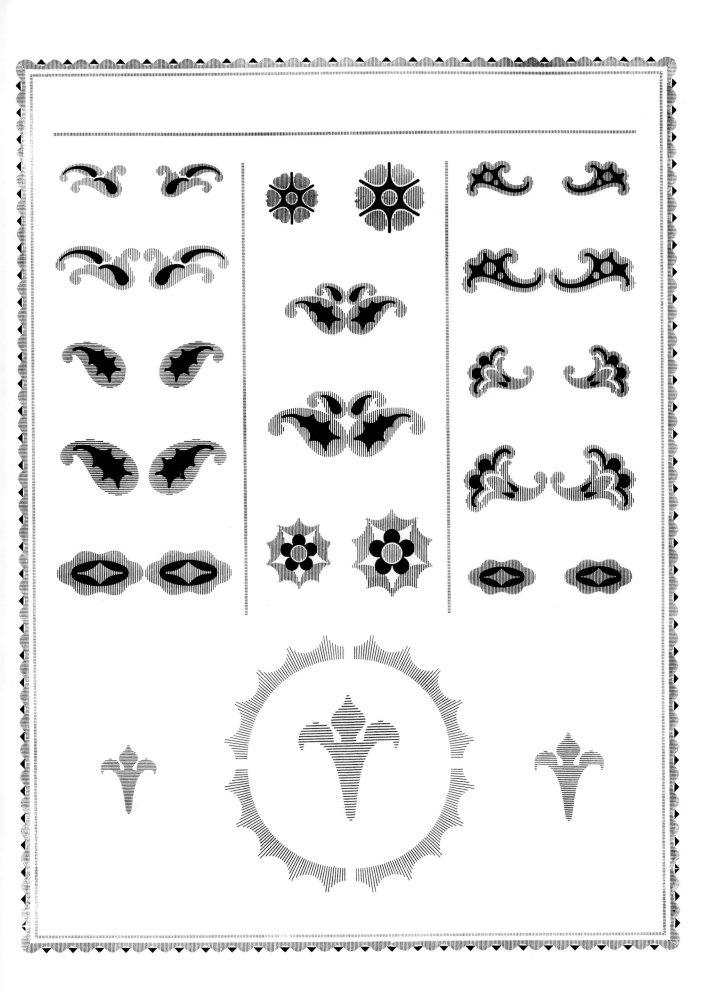

137

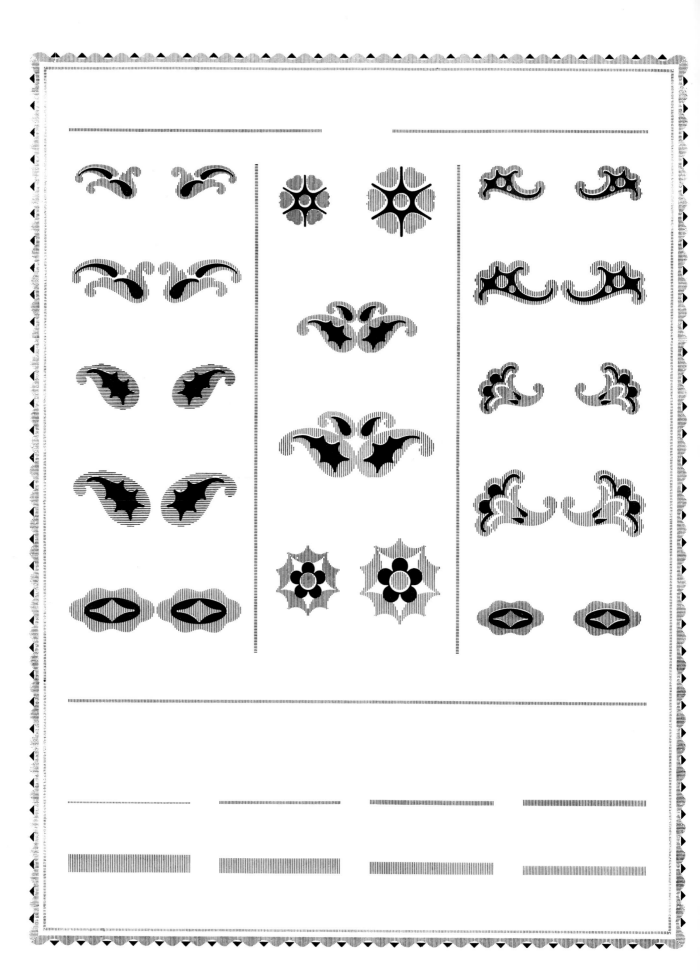

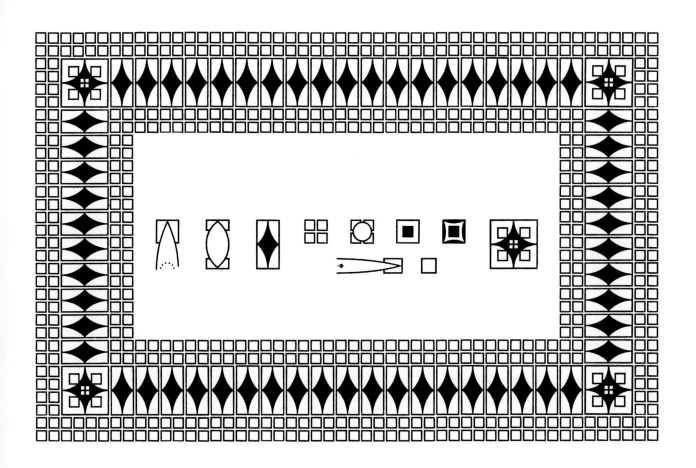

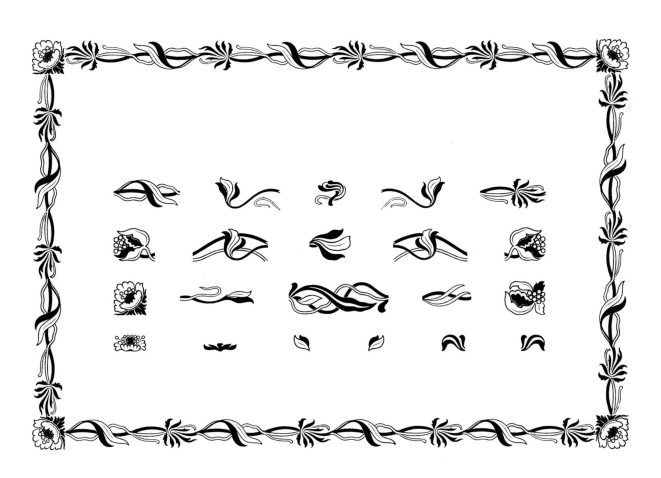

139

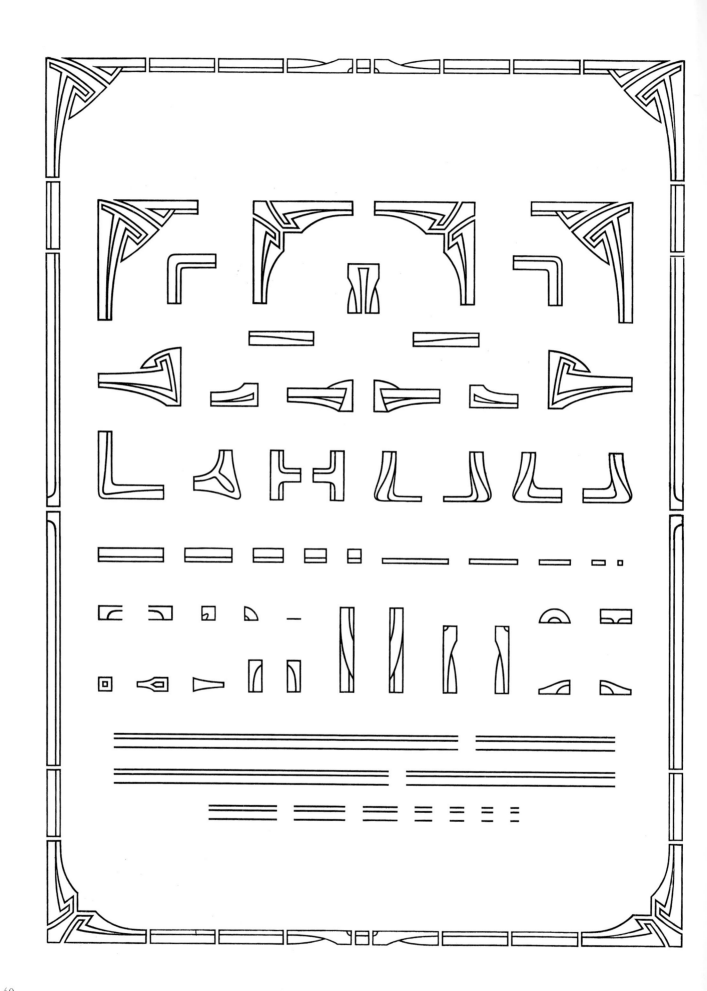

141

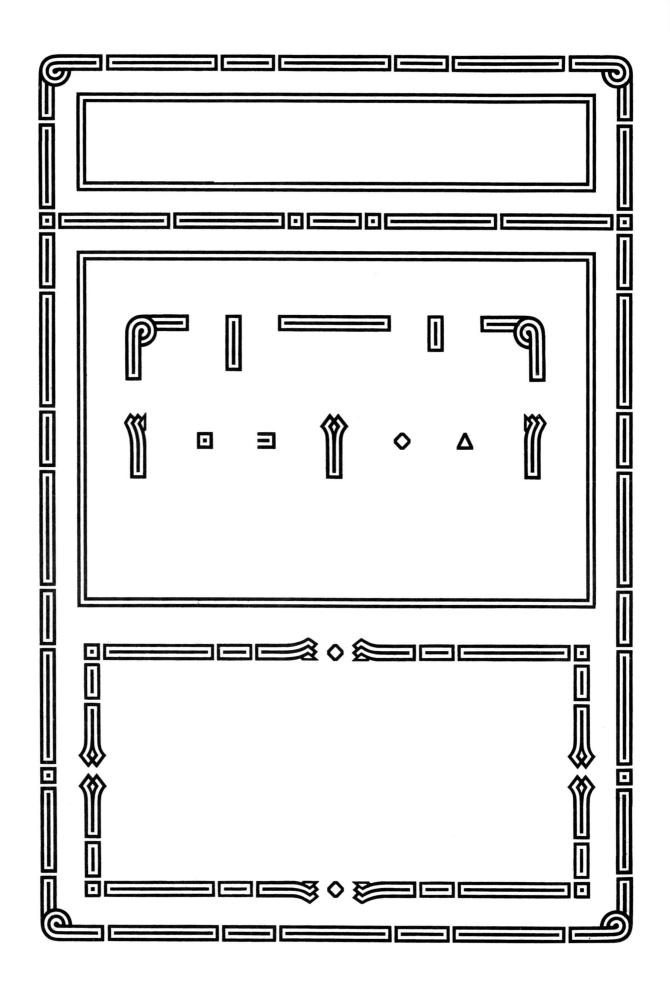

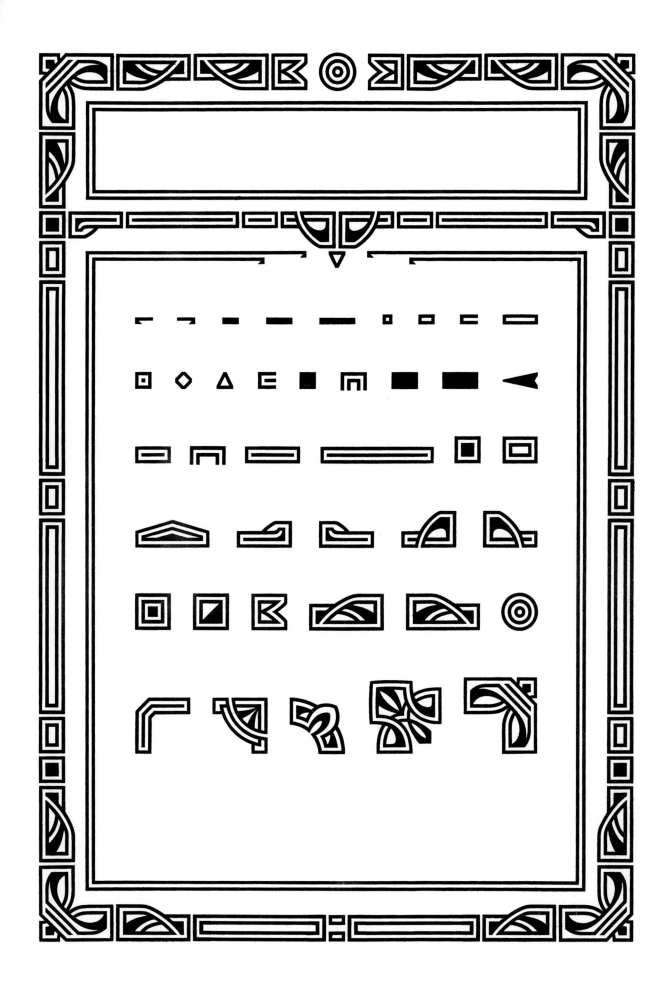

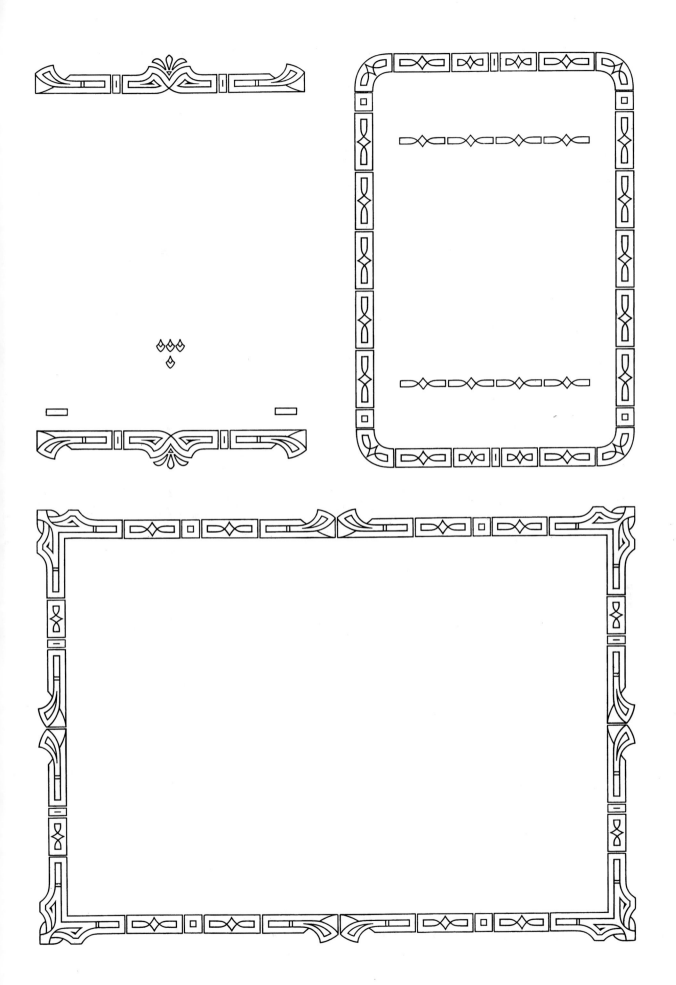

145

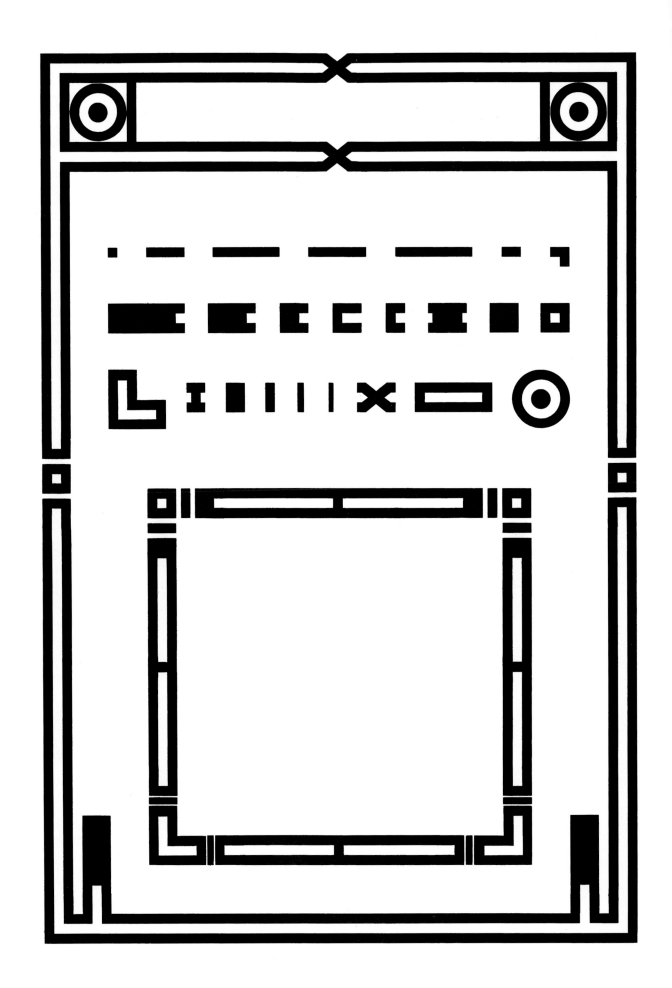

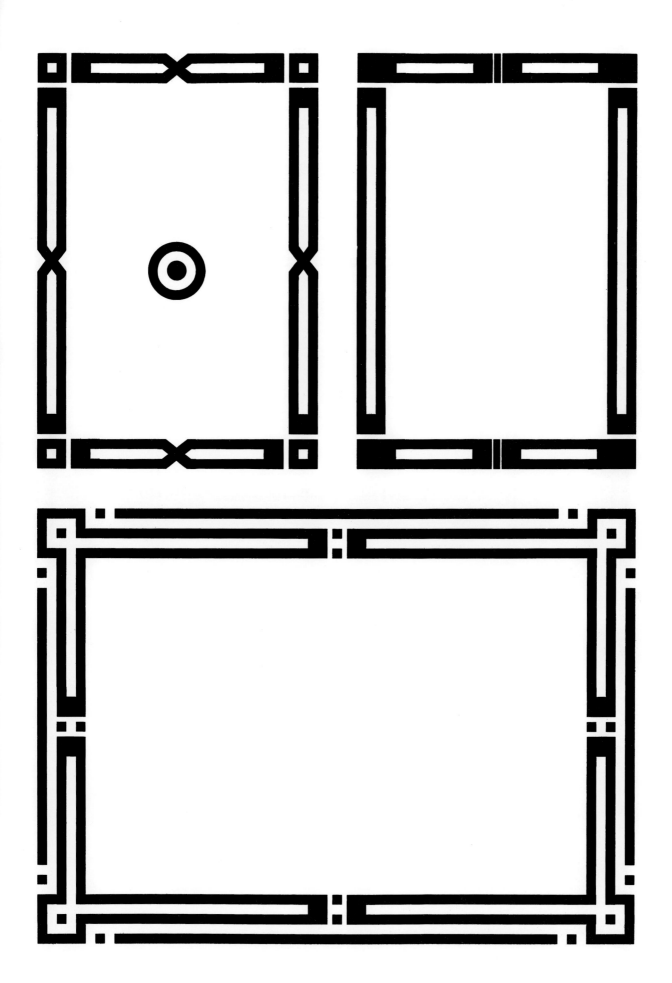

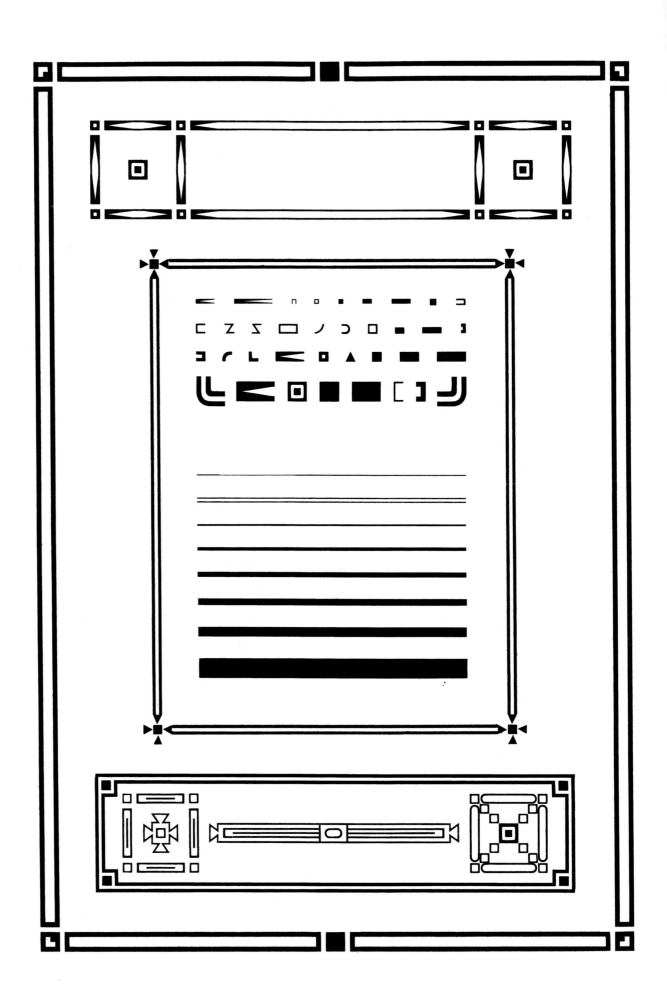

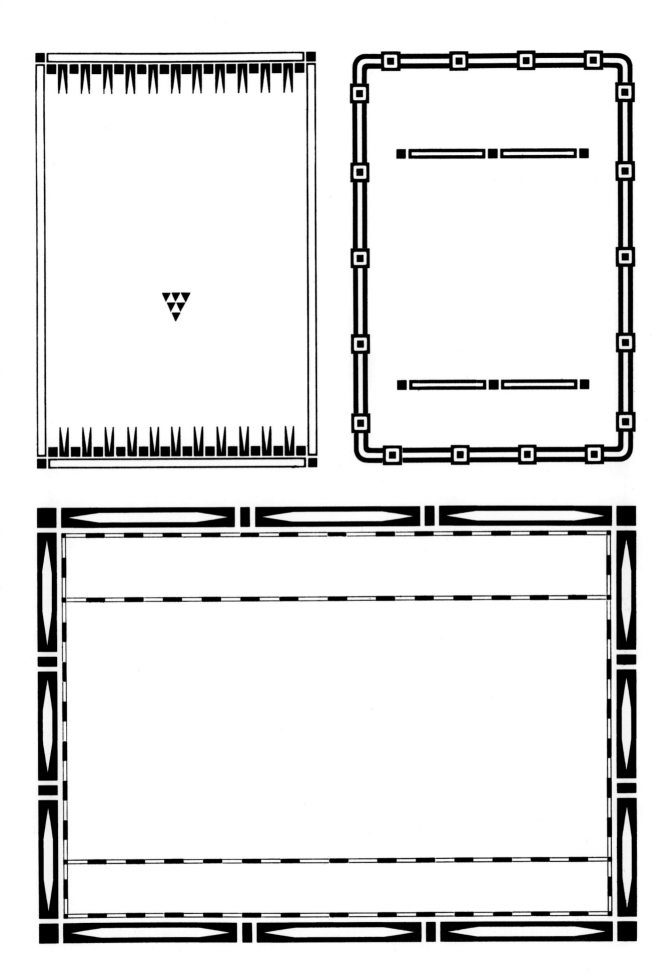

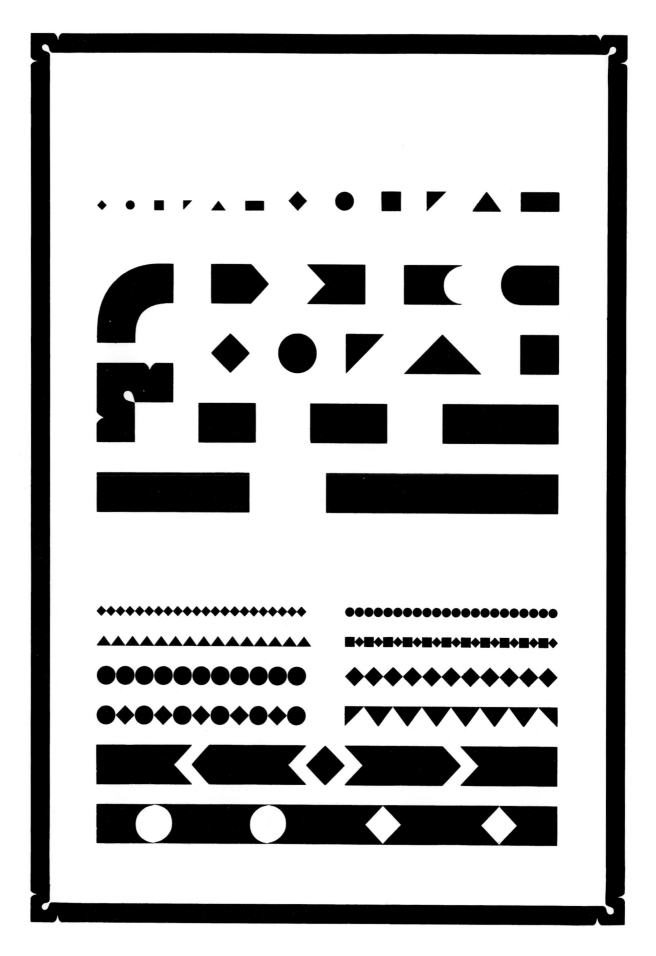

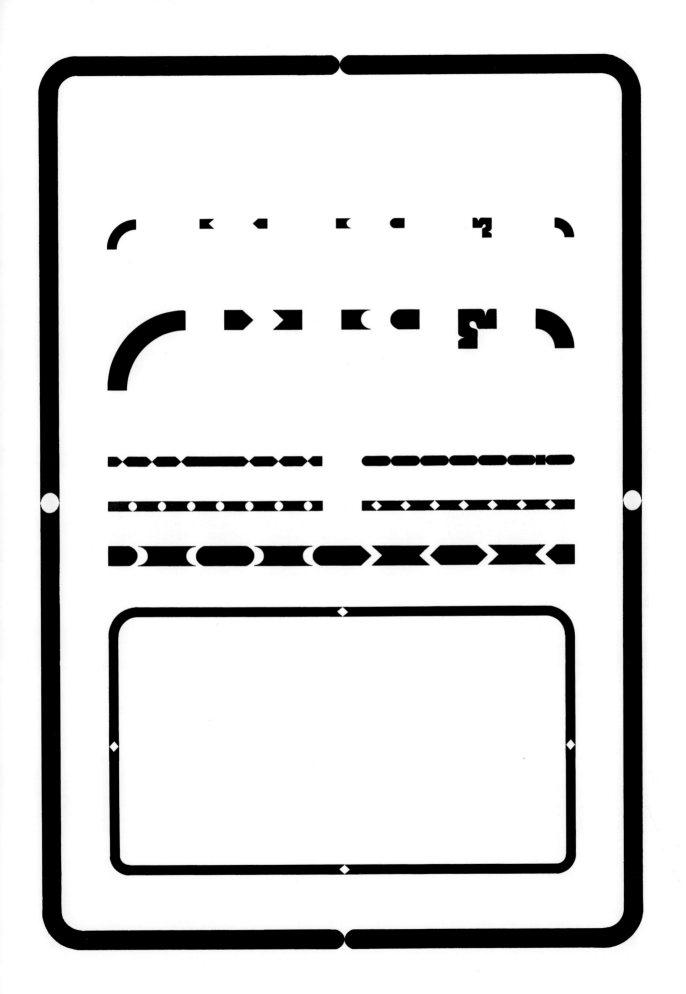

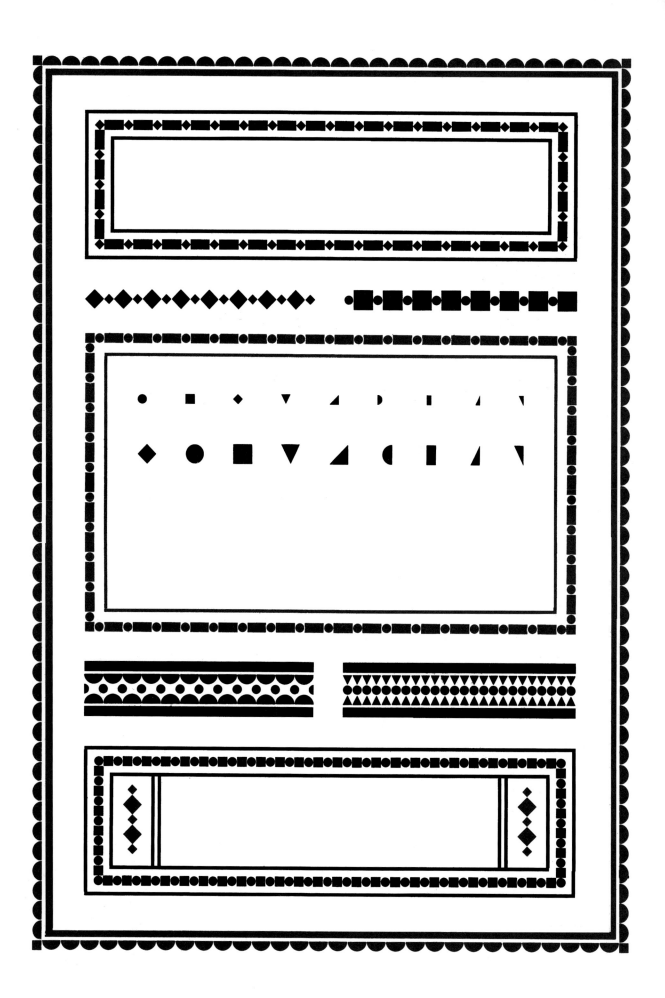

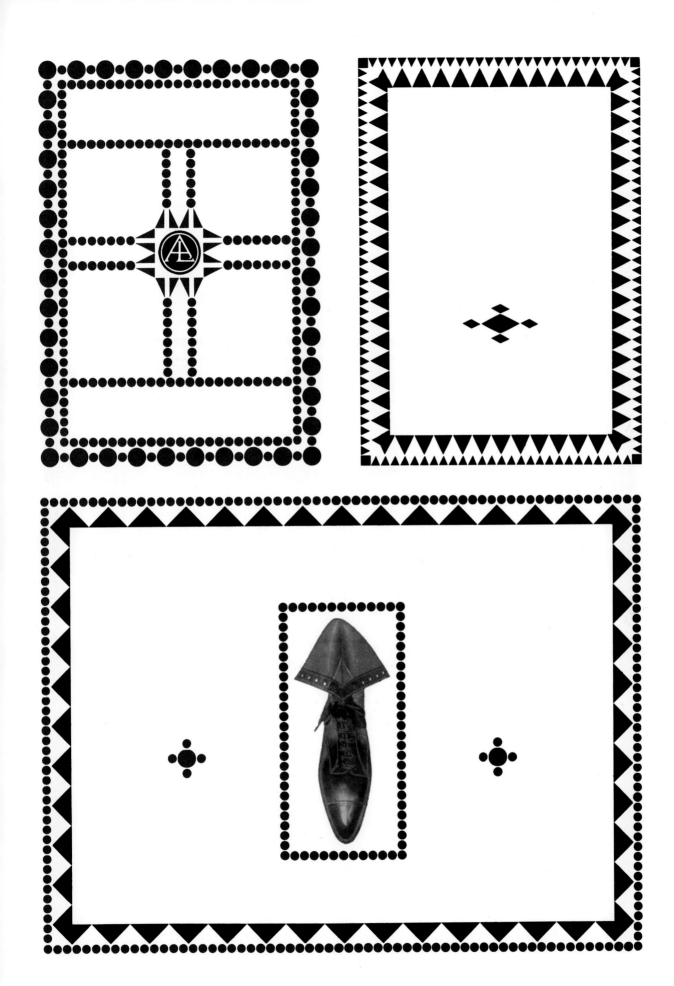

153

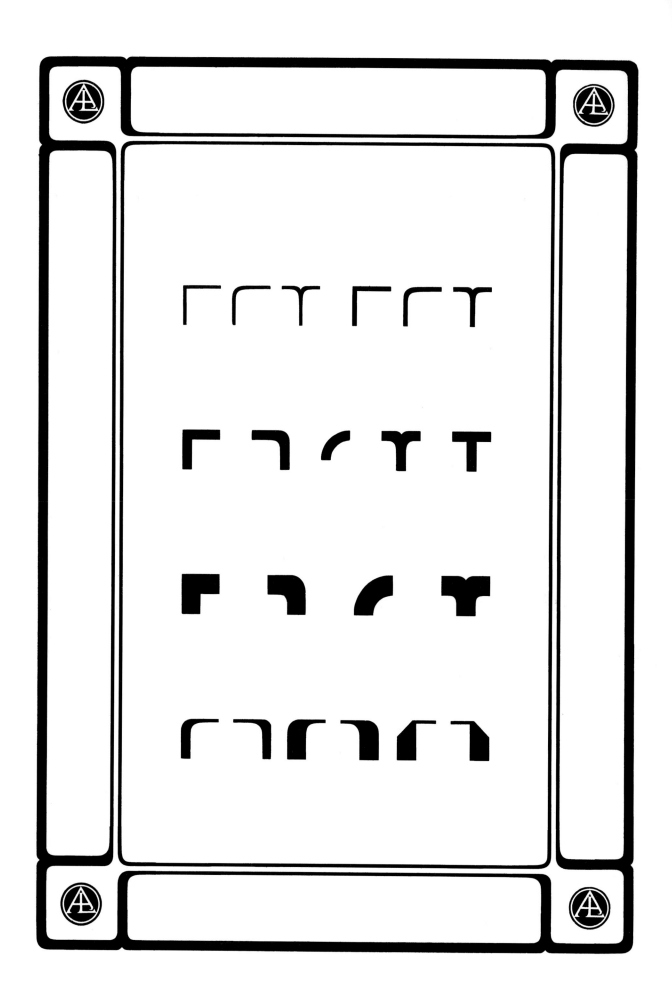

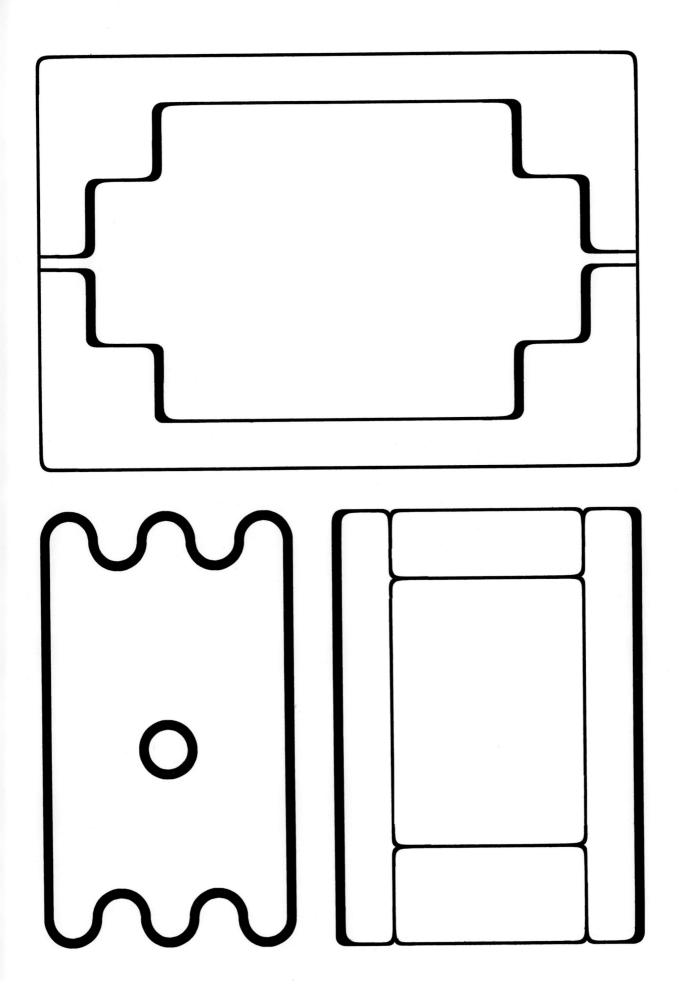

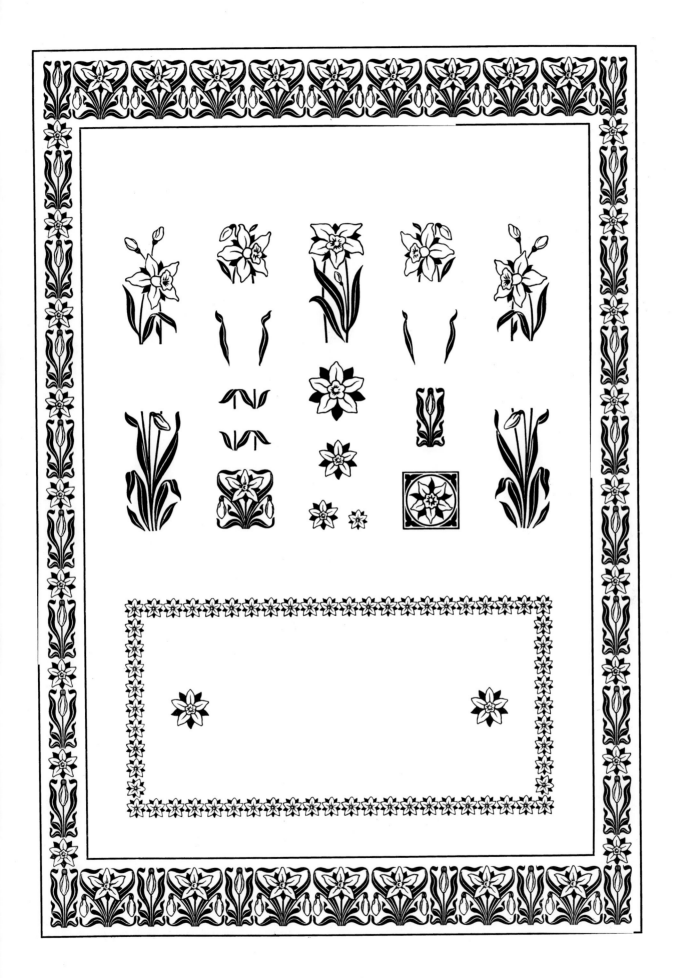

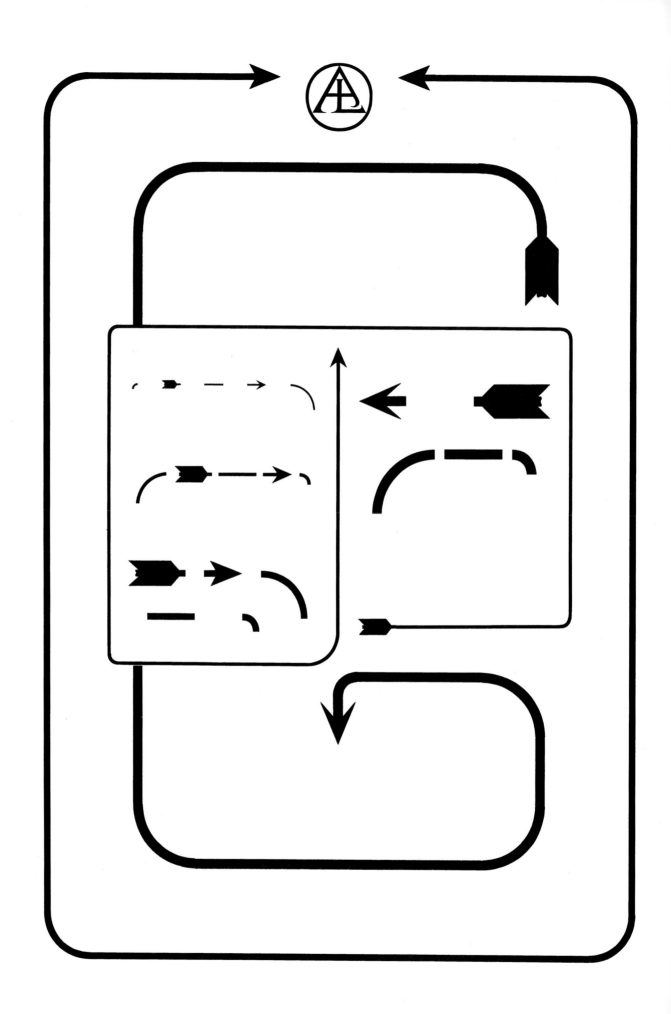

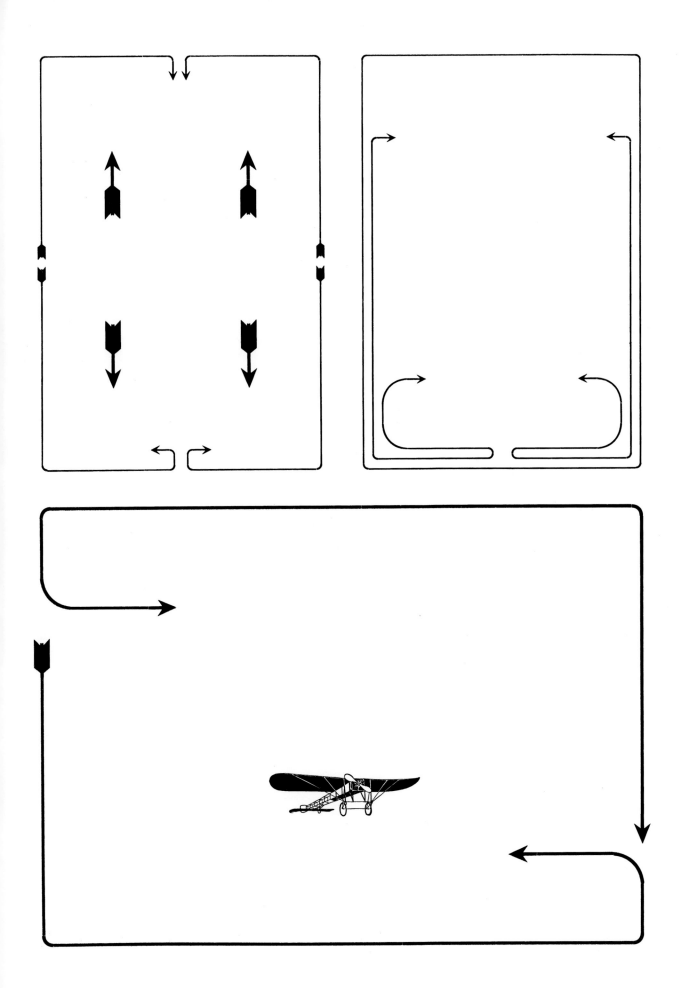

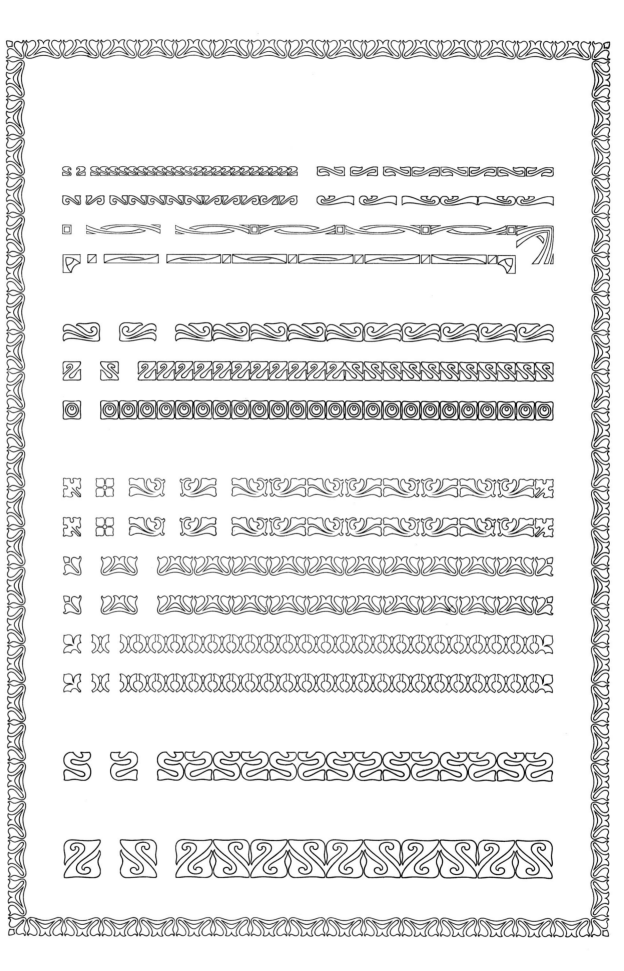

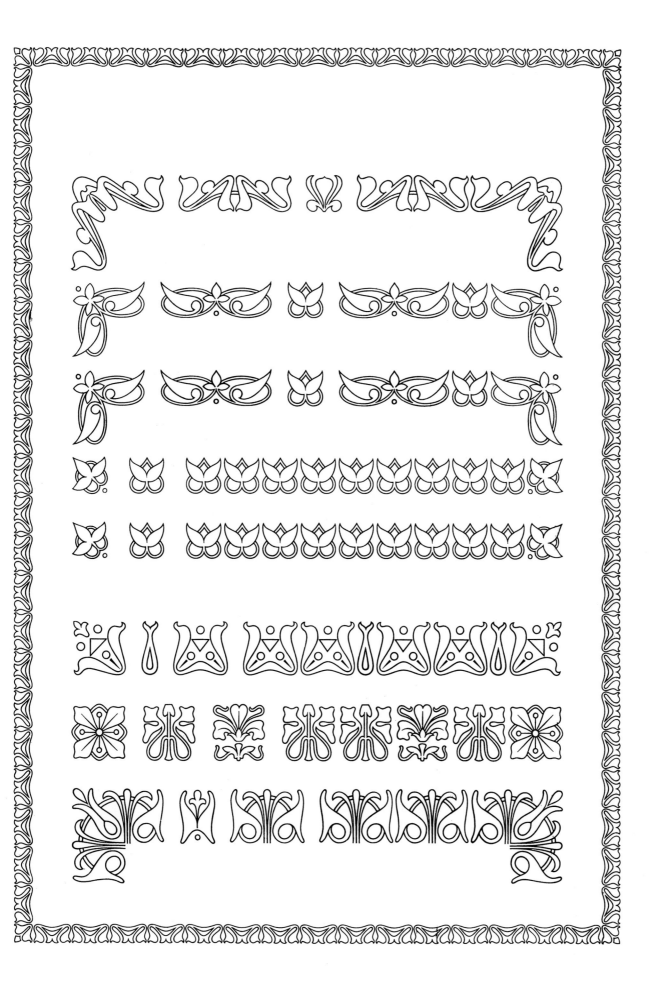

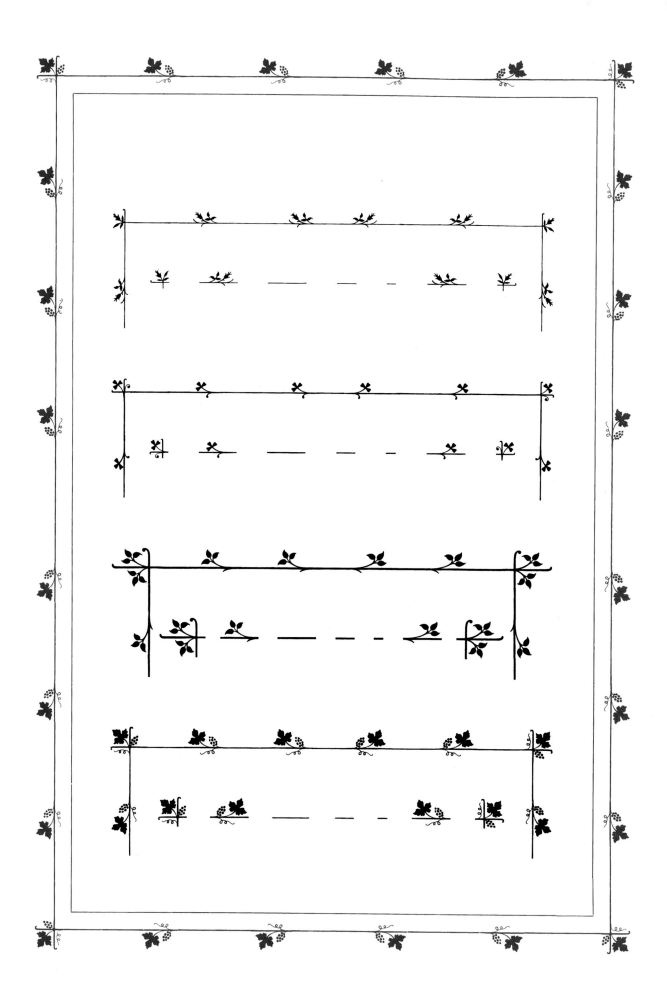

166

169

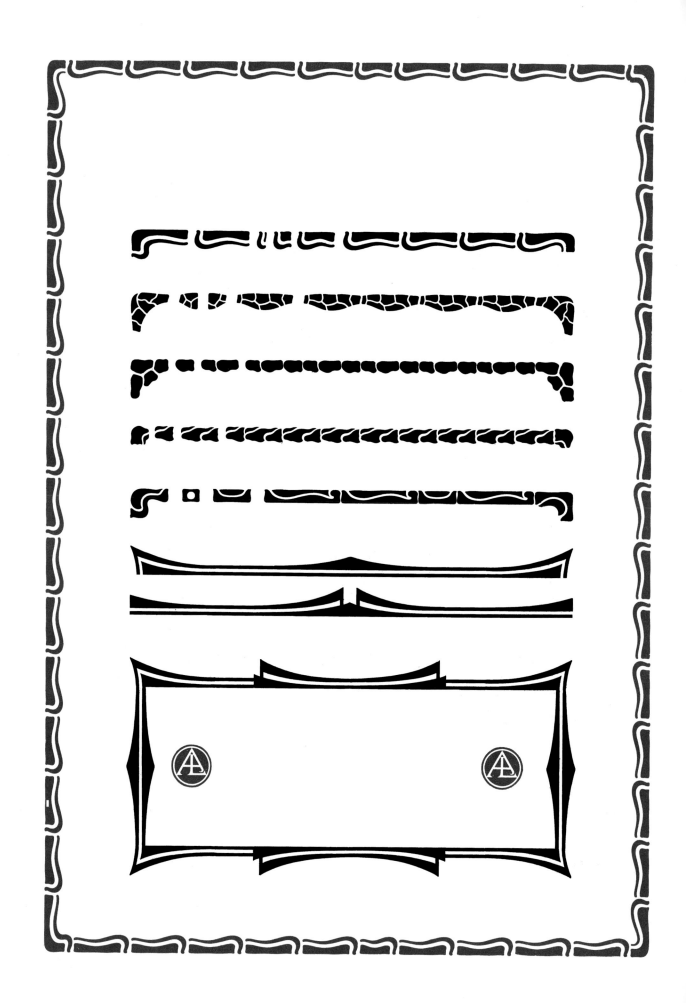

173

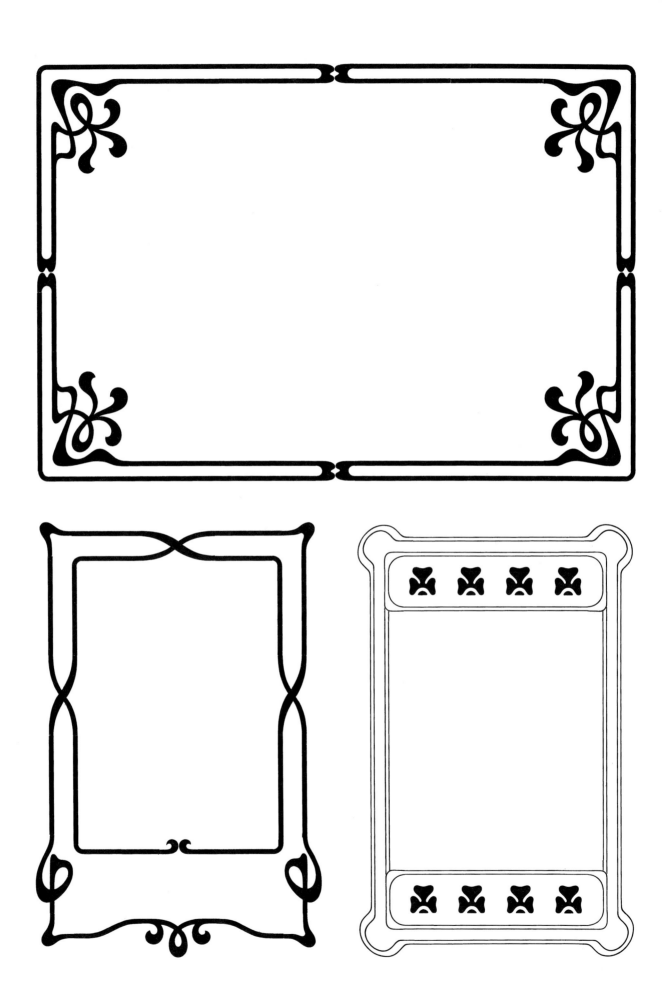

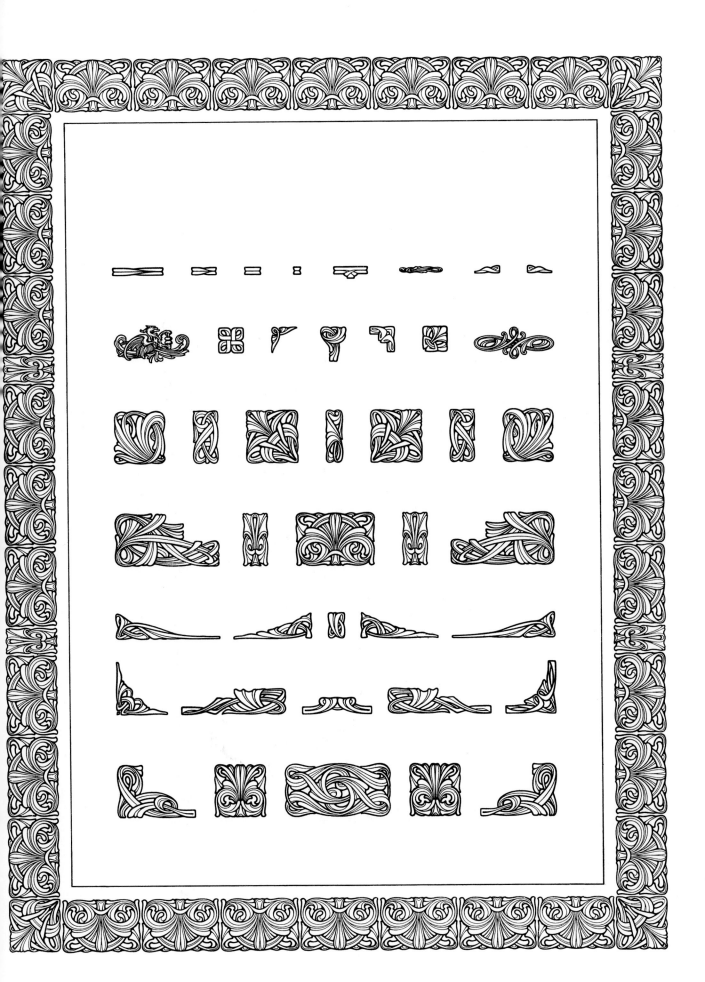

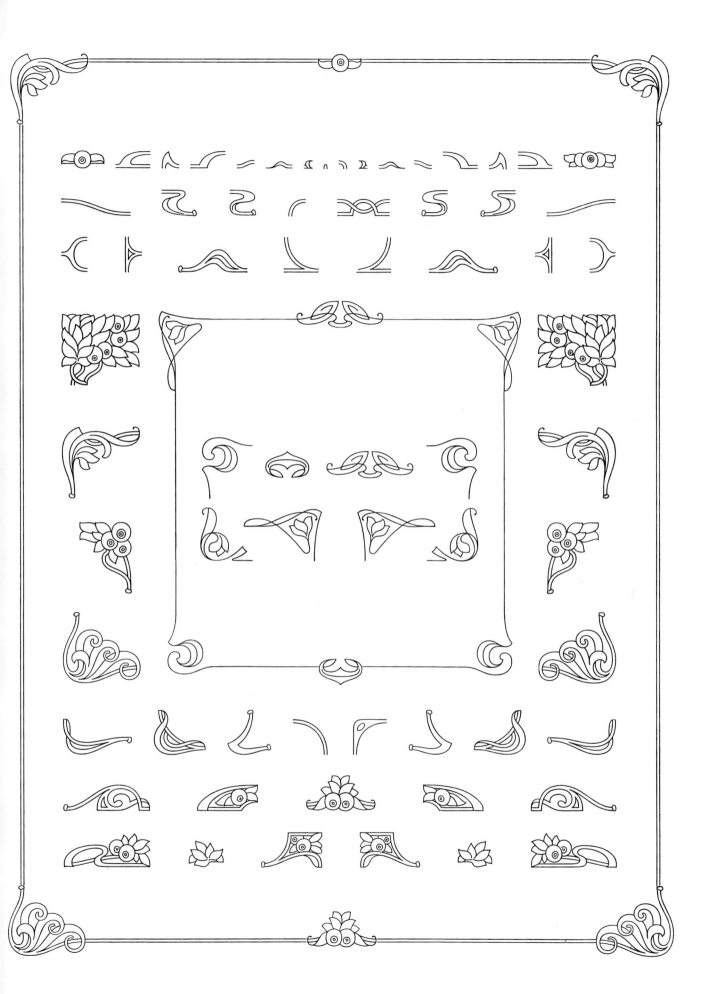

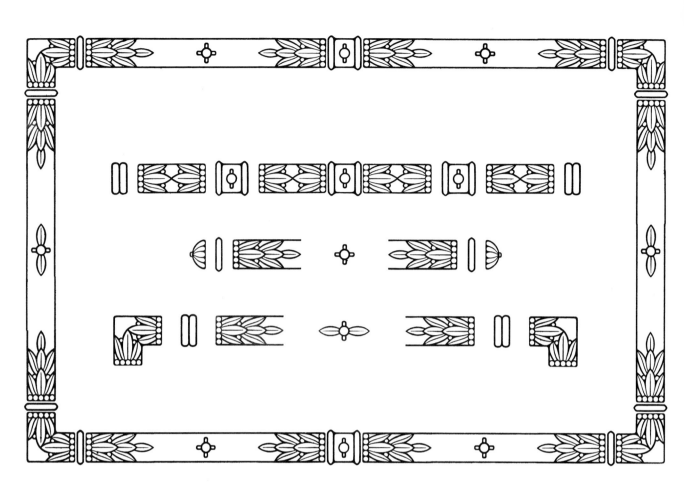

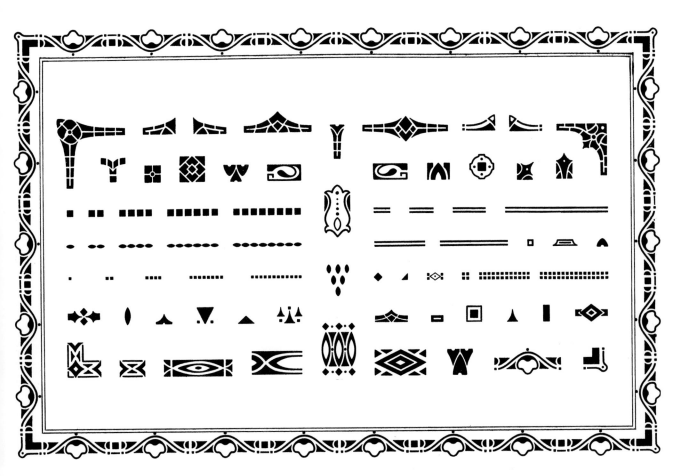

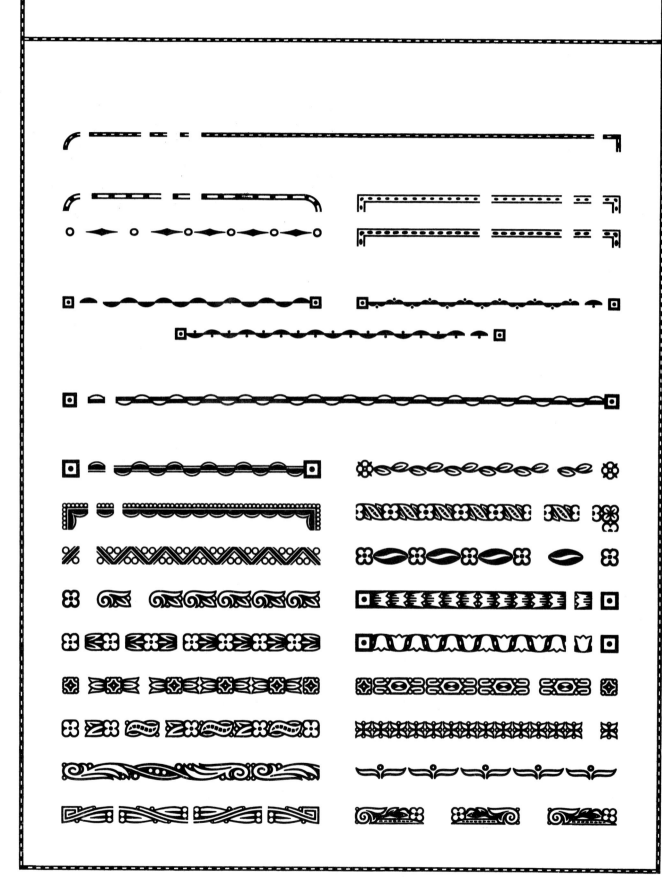

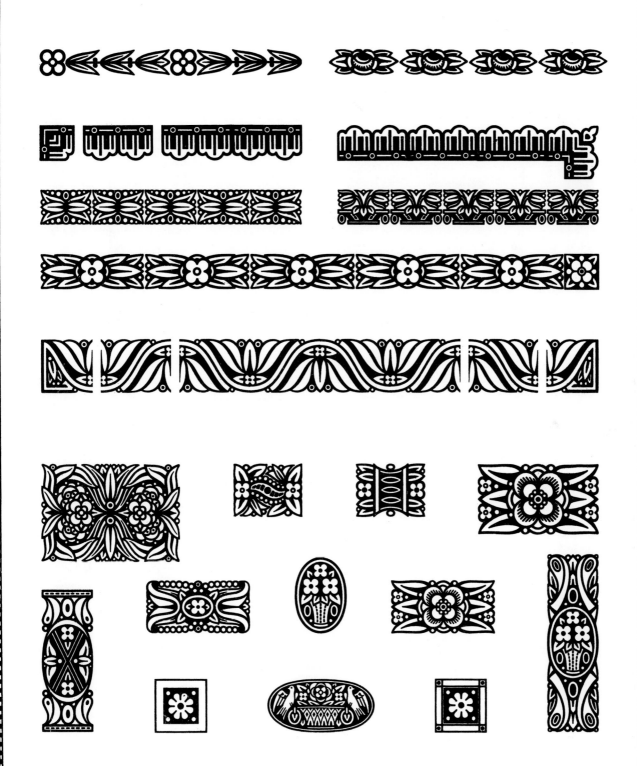

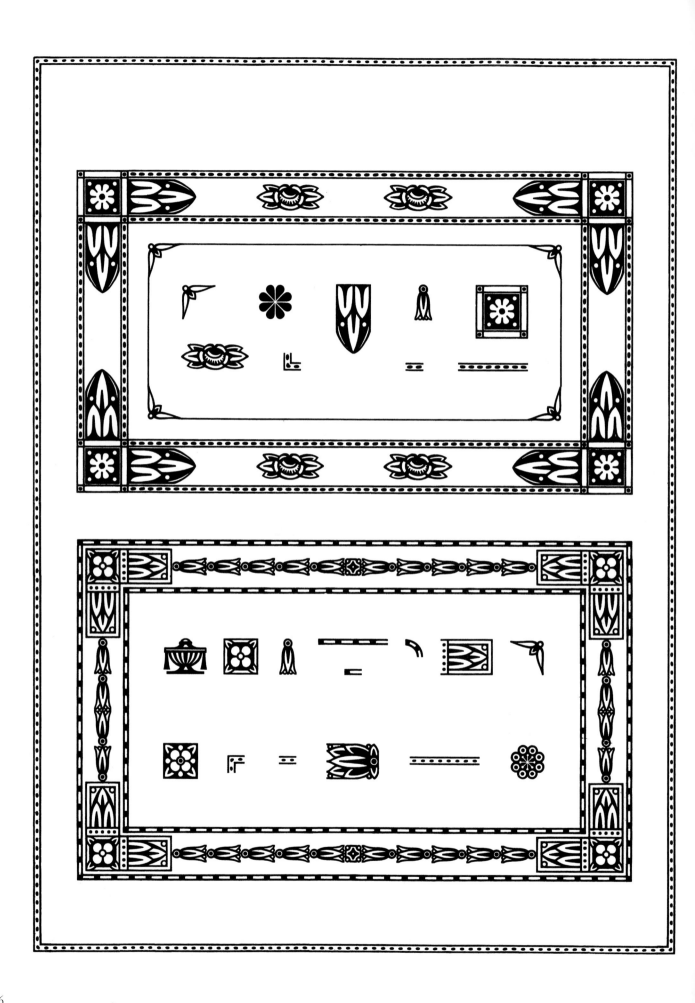

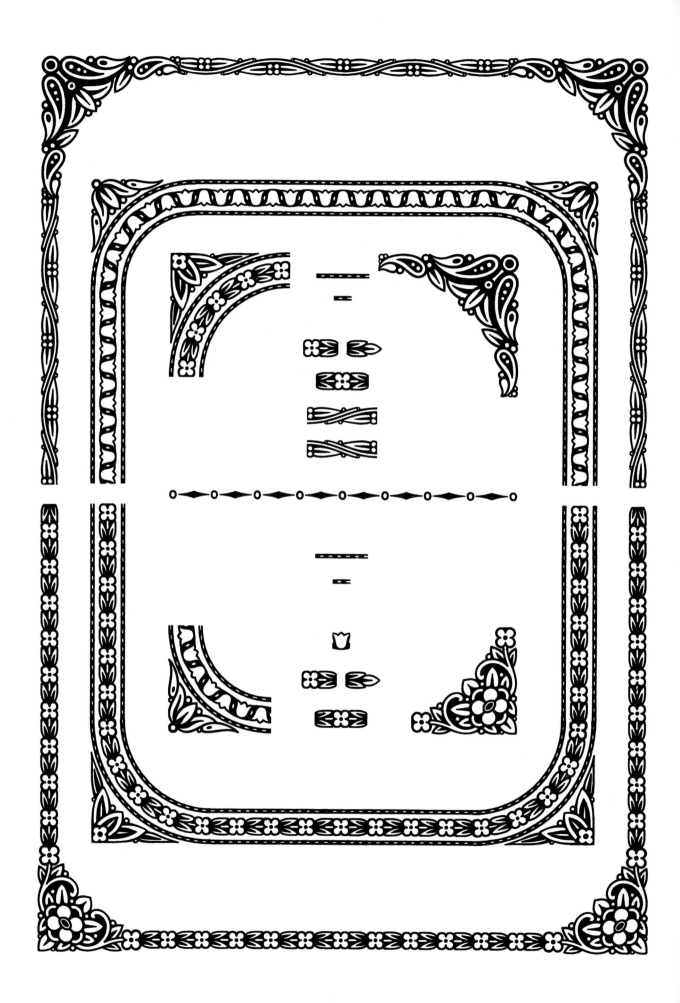

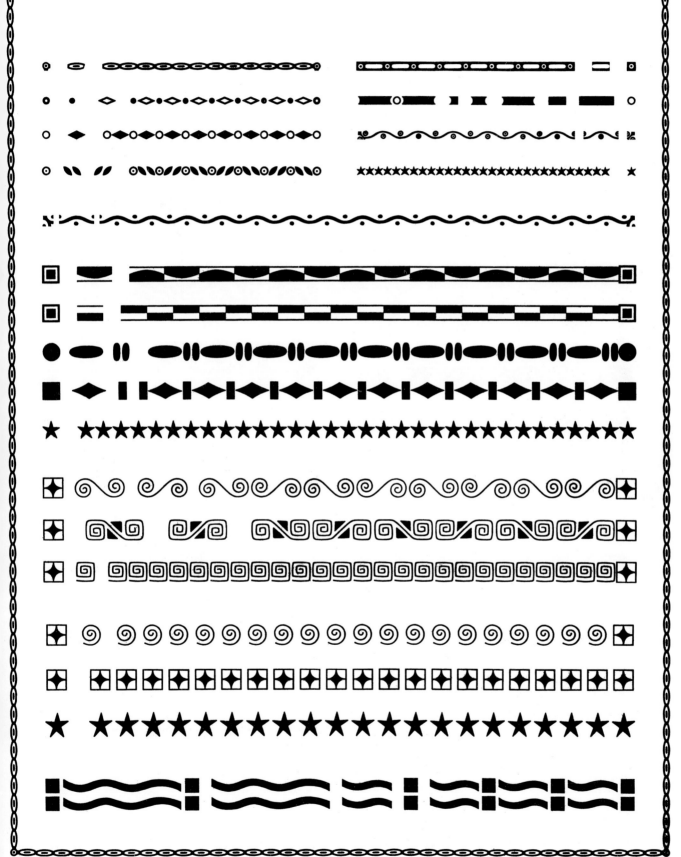

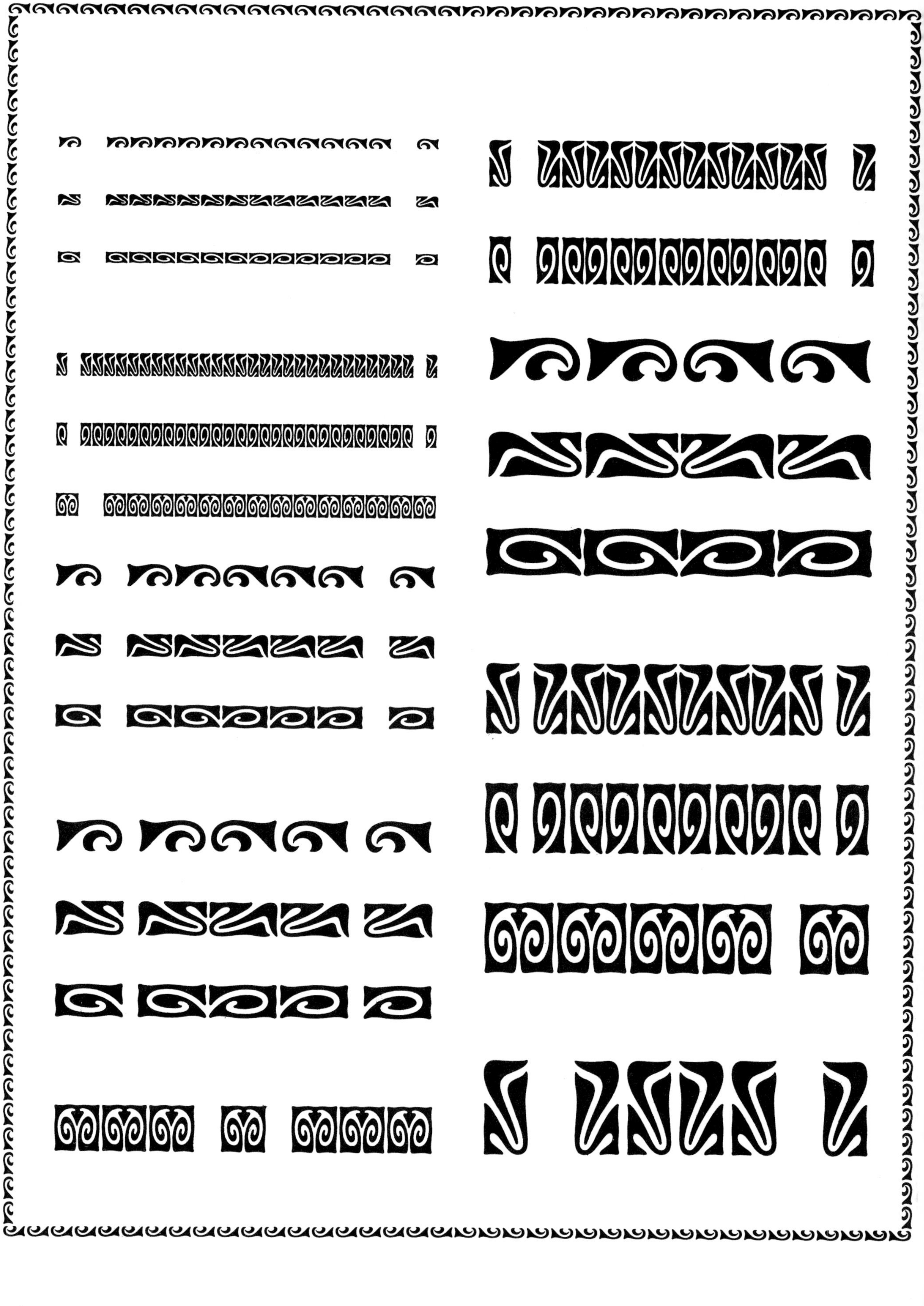

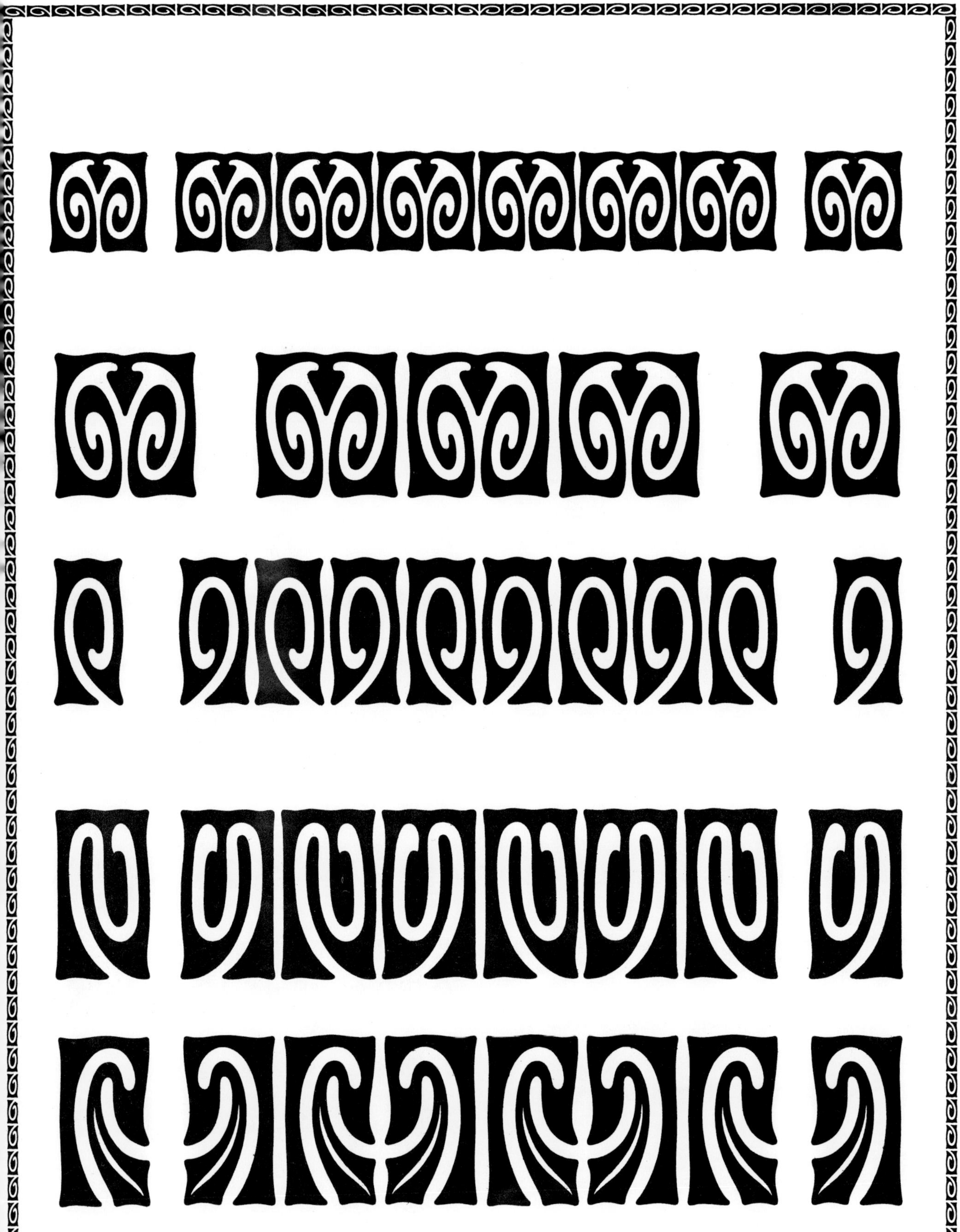

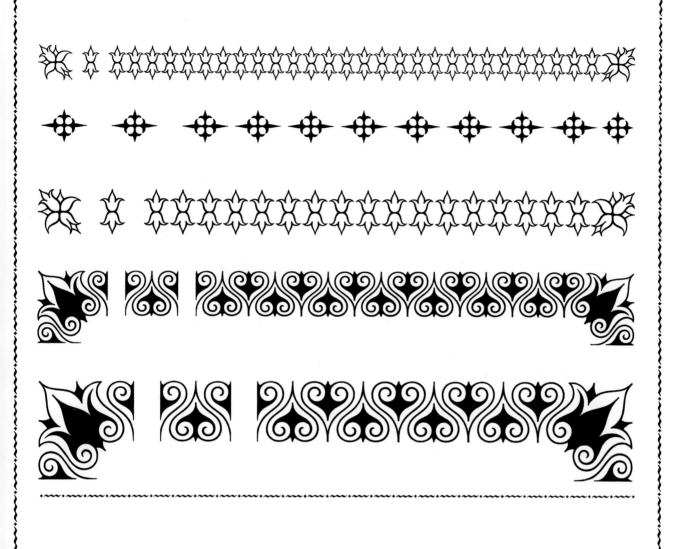

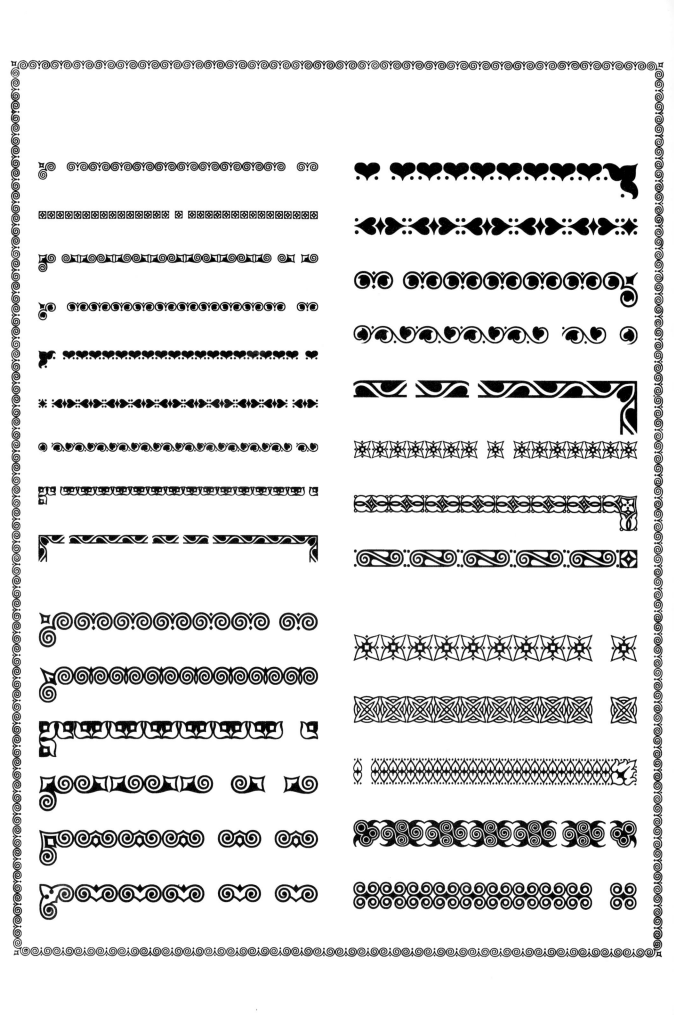

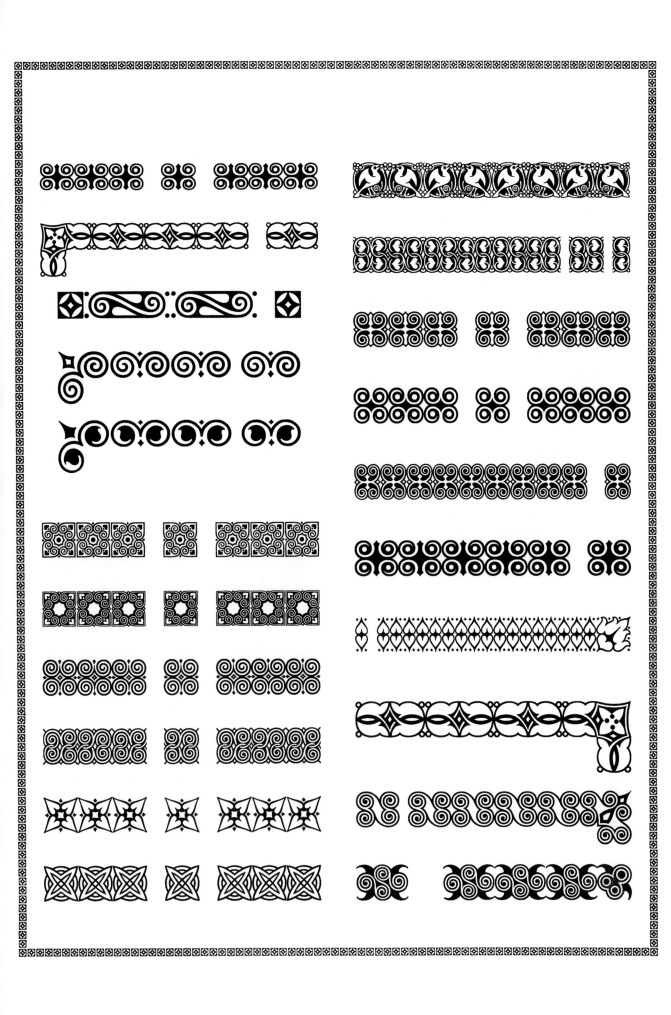

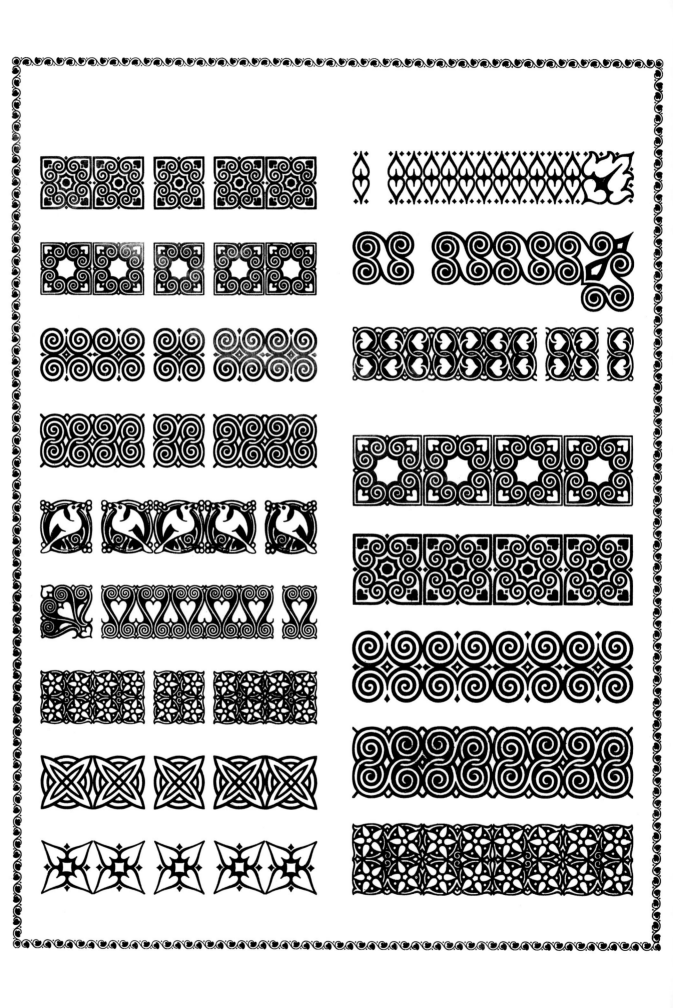

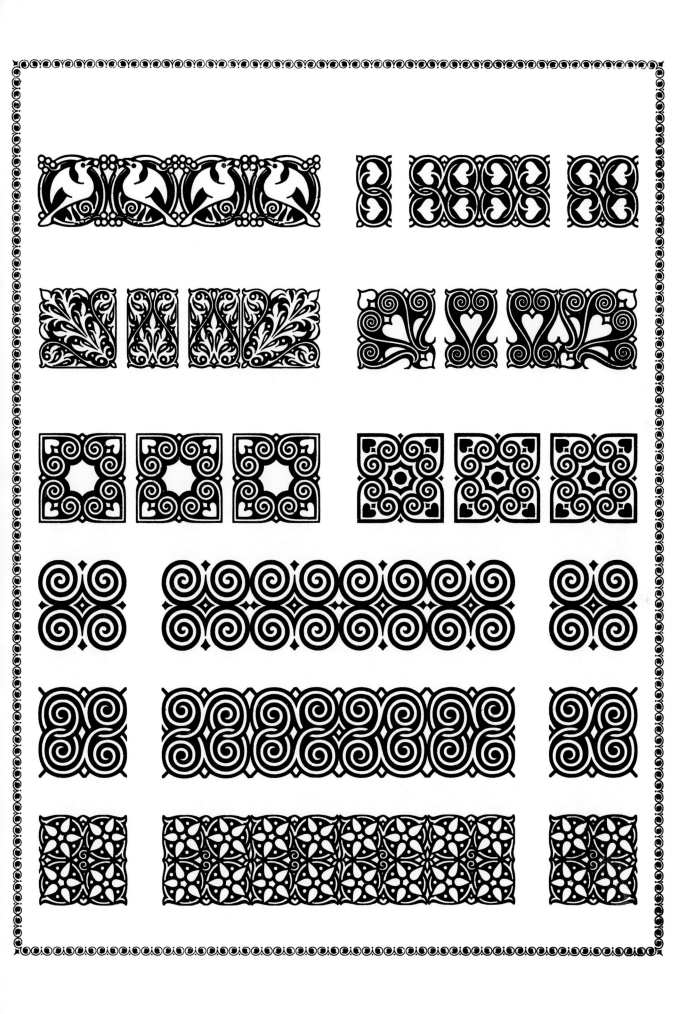

197

198

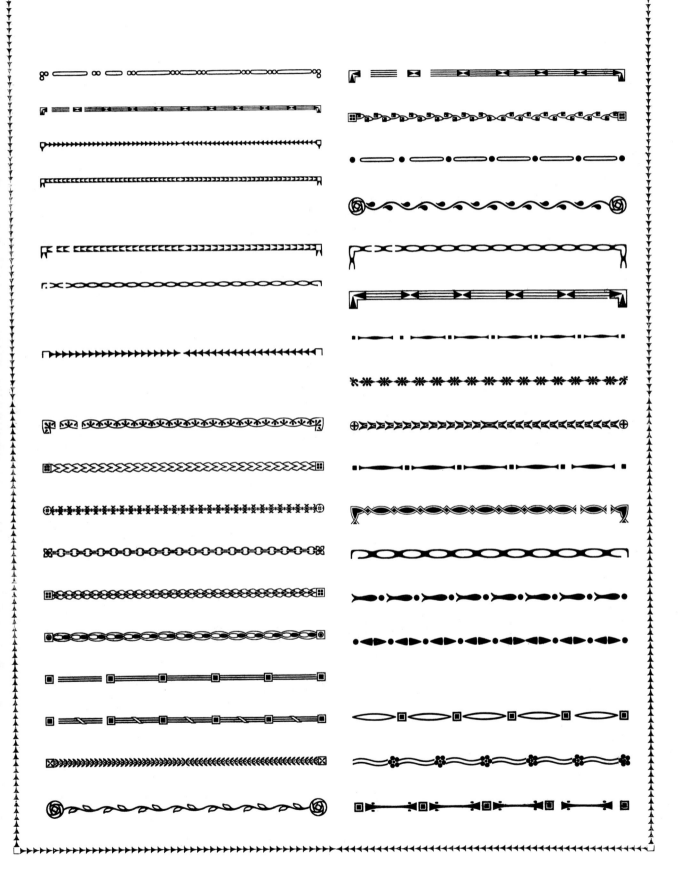

199

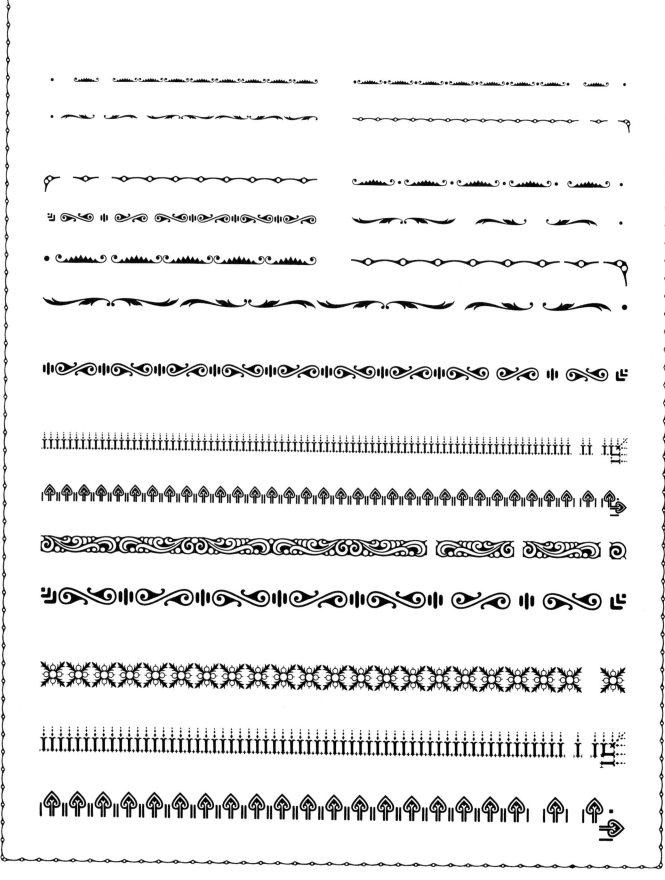

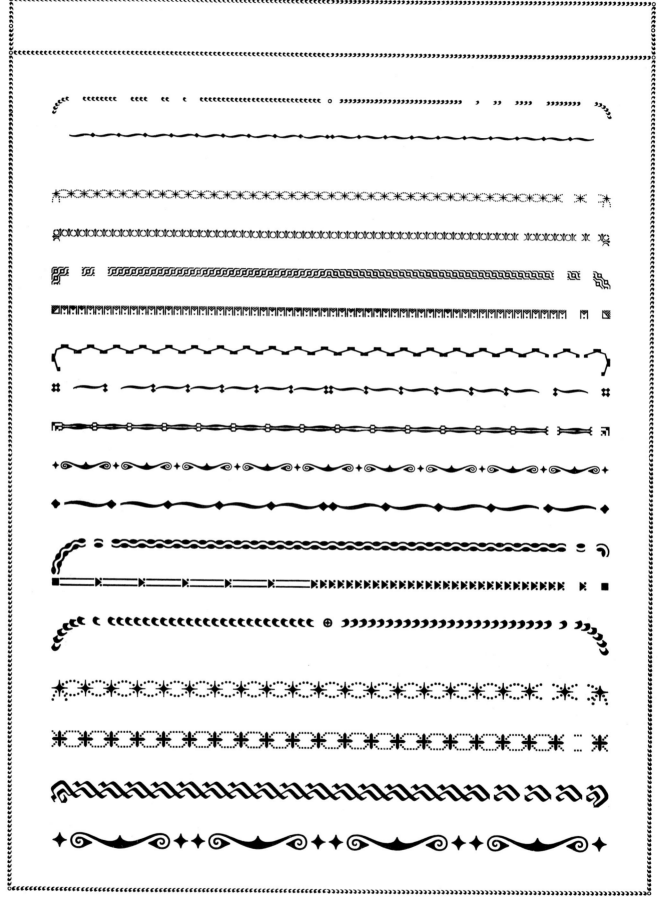

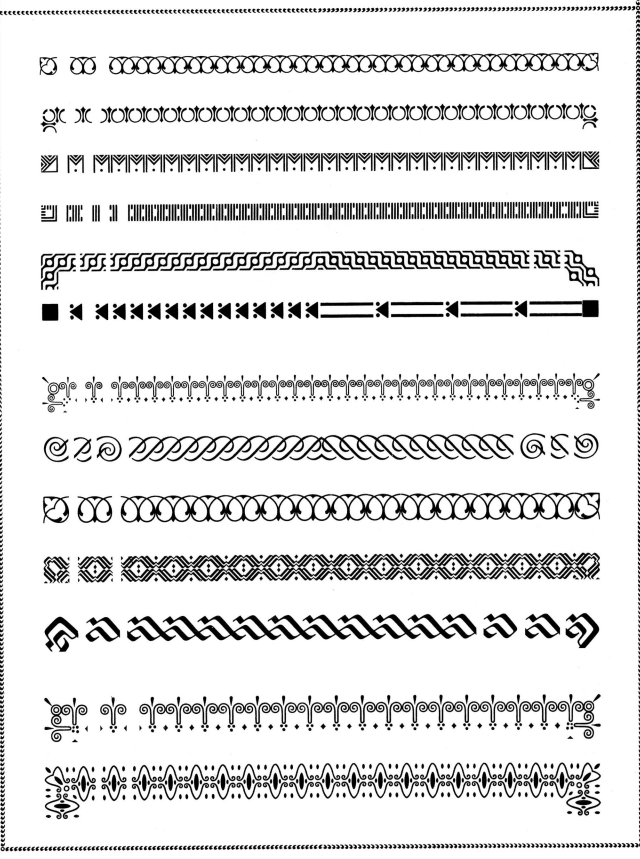

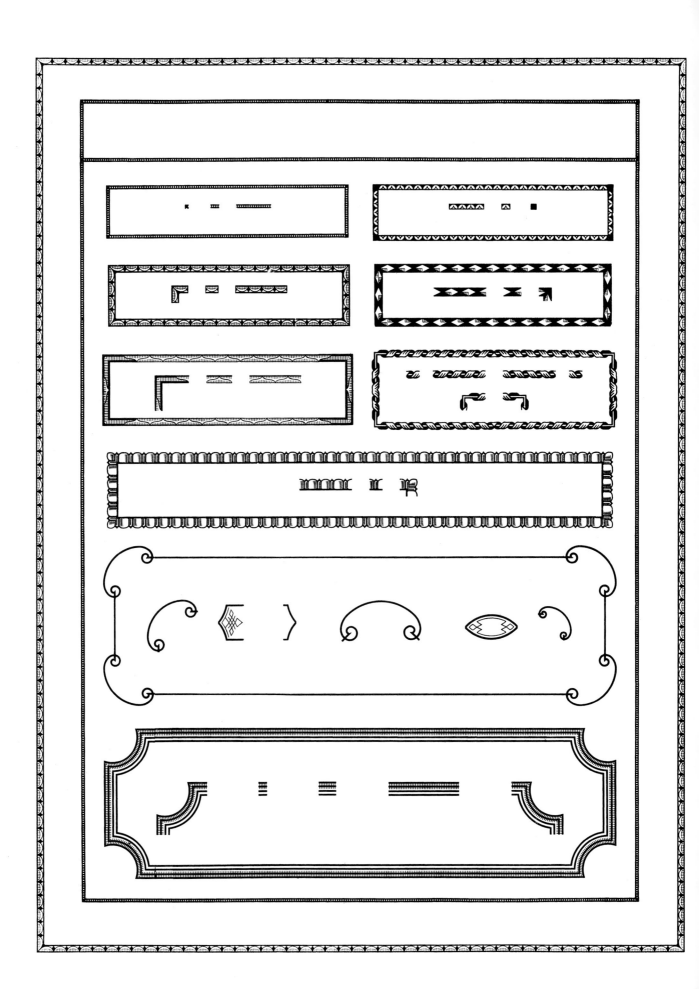

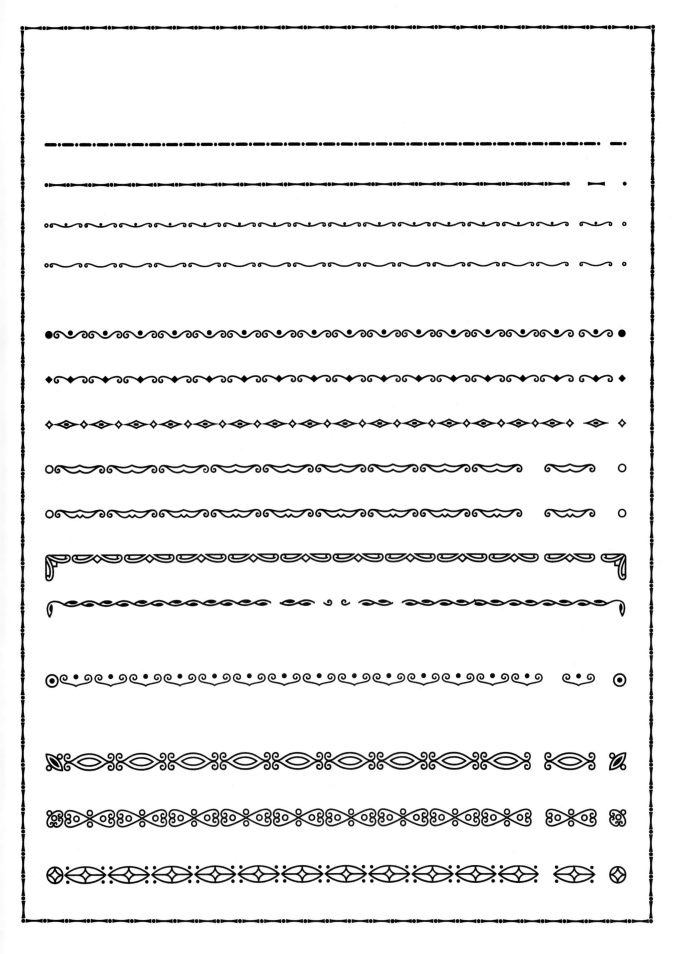

211

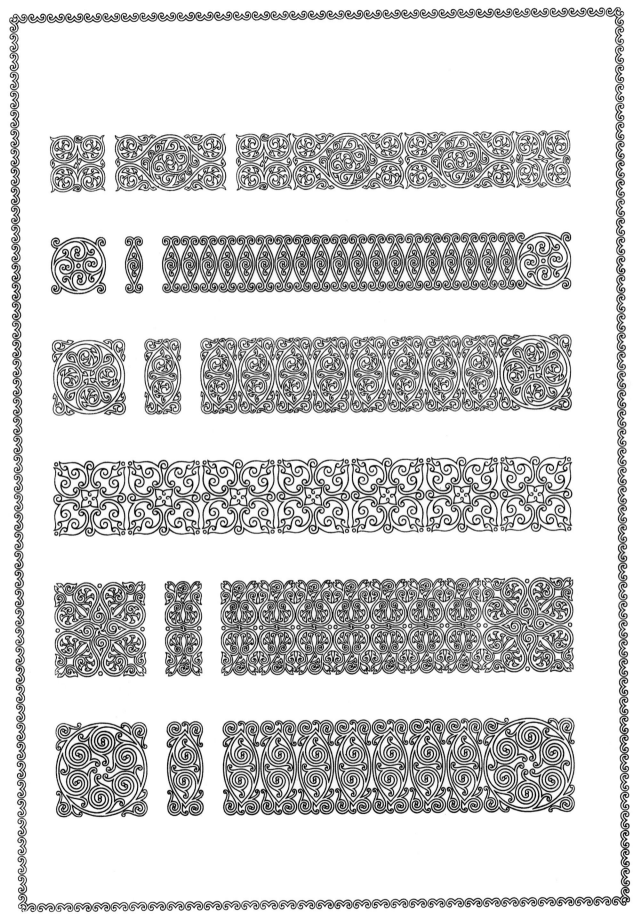

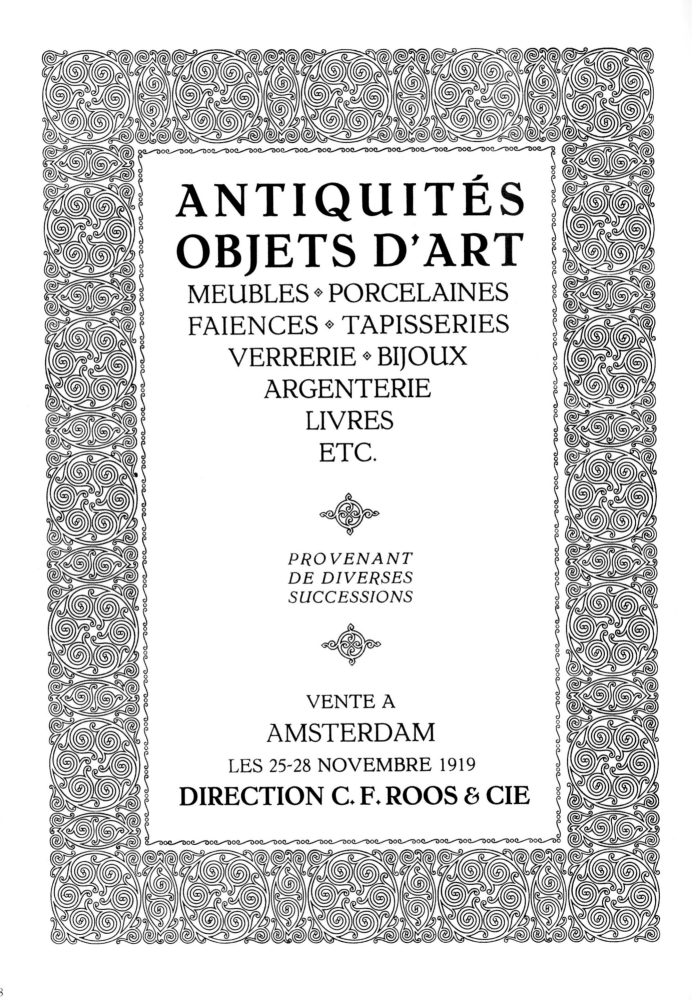

ANTIQUITÉS
OBJETS D'ART

MEUBLES ◦ PORCELAINES
FAIENCES ◦ TAPISSERIES
VERRERIE ◦ BIJOUX
ARGENTERIE
LIVRES
ETC.

*PROVENANT
DE DIVERSES
SUCCESSIONS*

VENTE A

AMSTERDAM

LES 25-28 NOVEMBRE 1919

DIRECTION C. F. ROOS & CIE

219

222

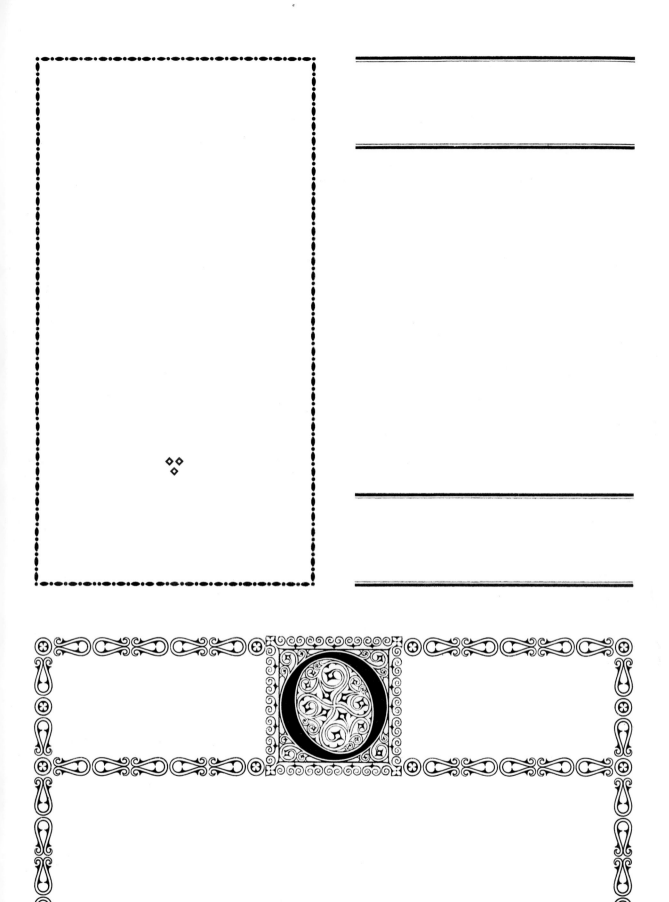

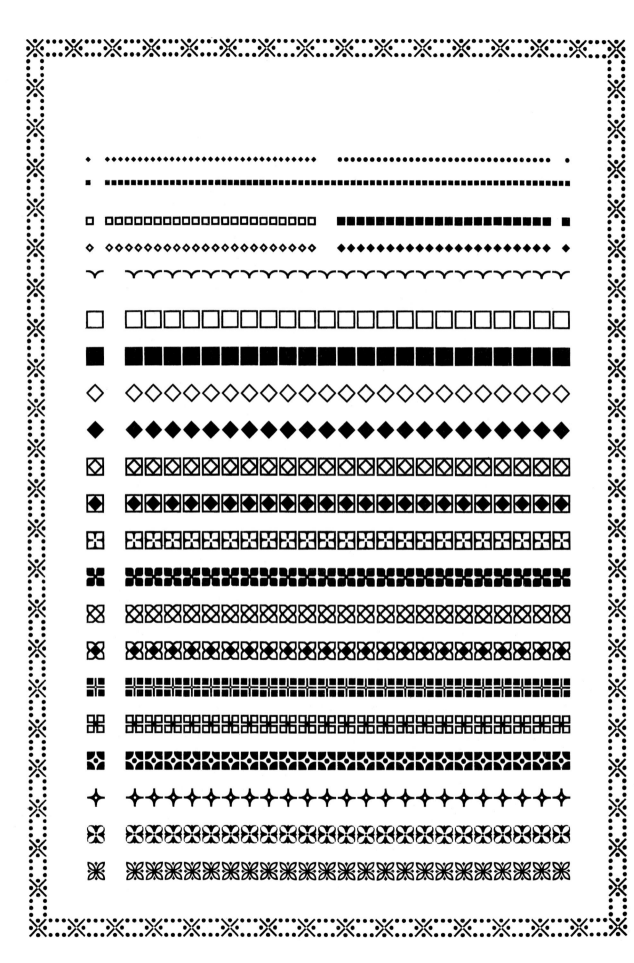

225

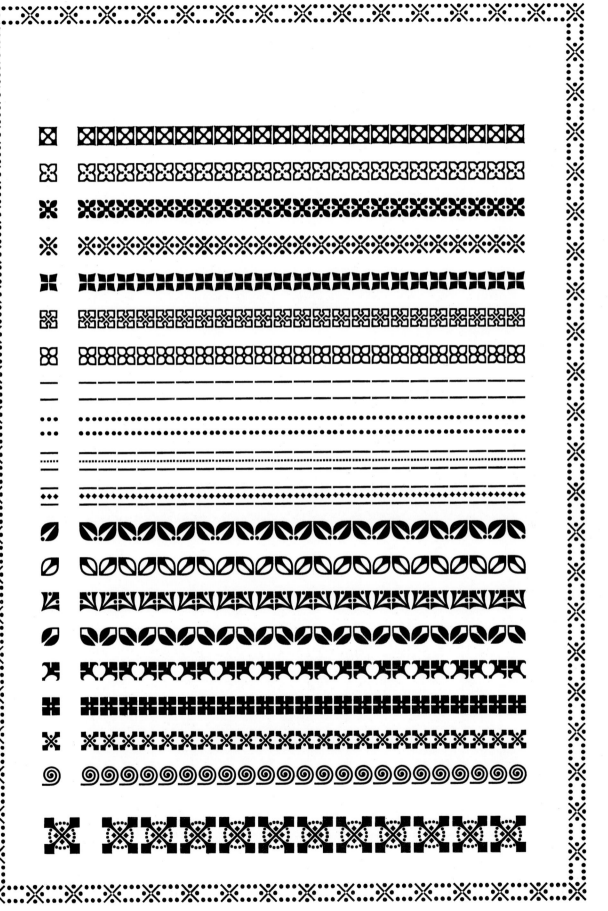

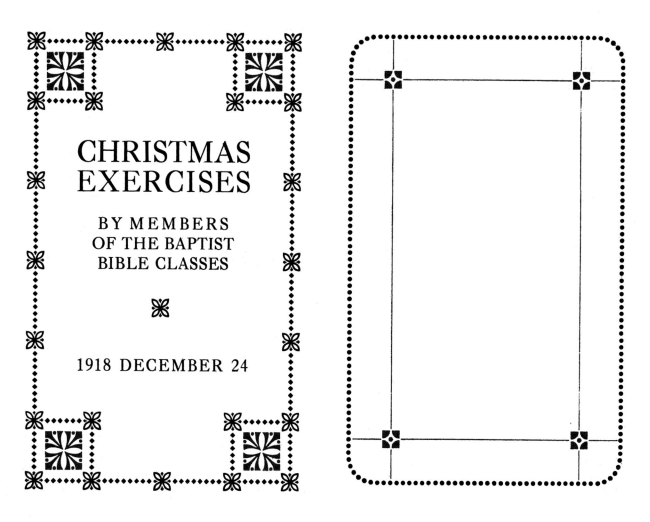

CHRISTMAS EXERCISES

BY MEMBERS
OF THE BAPTIST
BIBLE CLASSES

❋

1918 DECEMBER 24

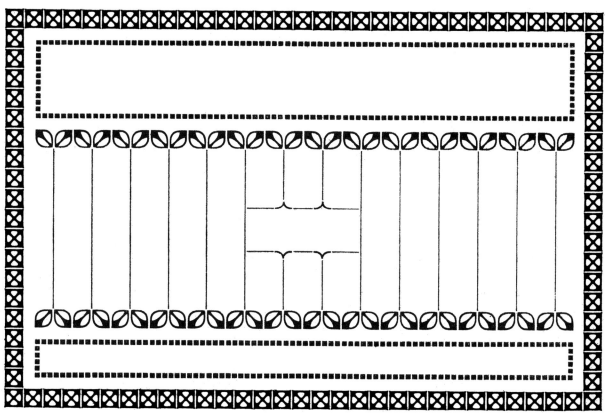

BALBOEKJE

18 DECEMBER 1916

DAM-HOTEL

MENU

Truites à la Bordelaise

Poulets nouveaux aux pois

Buisson de foie gras en belle-veu

Selle de chevreuil sauce poivrade

Asperges en branches

Fromages   Dessert

Per couvert minstens 50 cent
Consumptie verplicht

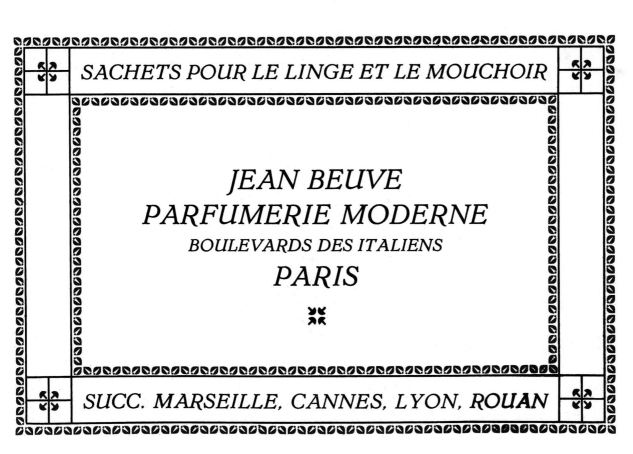

SACHETS POUR LE LINGE ET LE MOUCHOIR

JEAN BEUVE
PARFUMERIE MODERNE
BOULEVARDS DES ITALIENS
PARIS

SUCC. MARSEILLE, CANNES, LYON, ROUAN

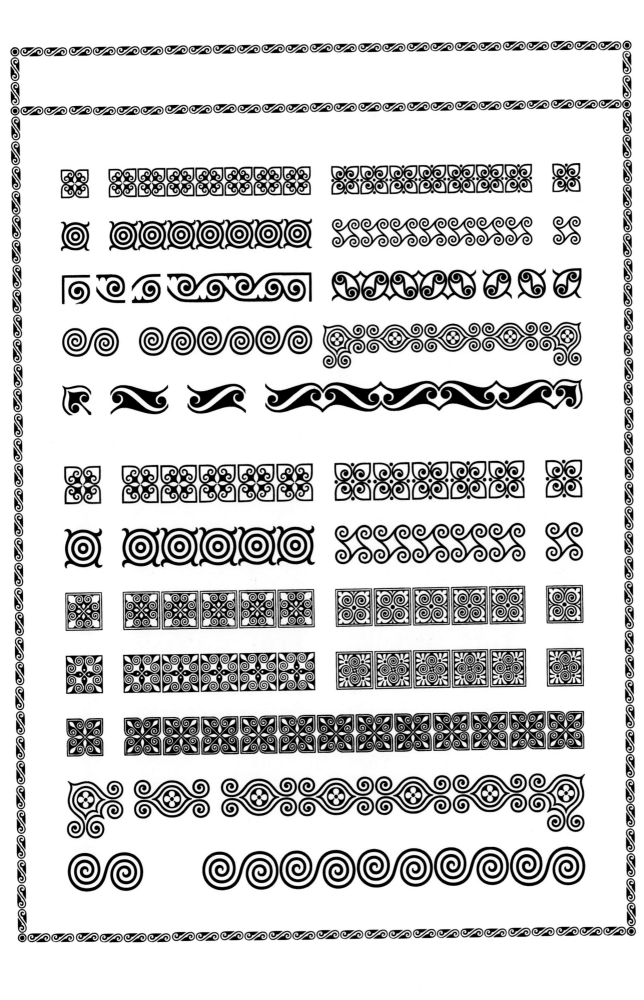

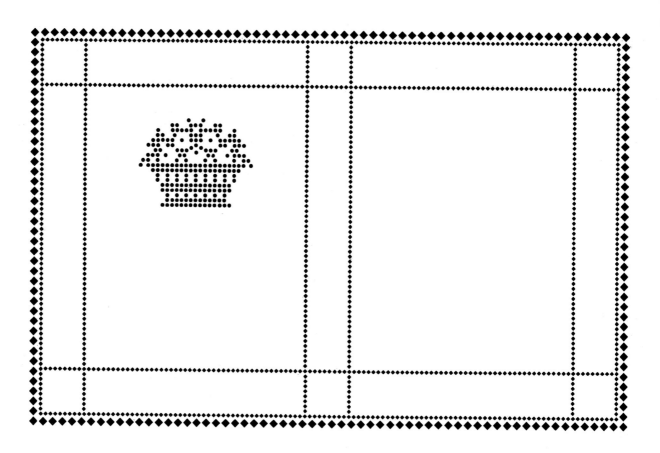

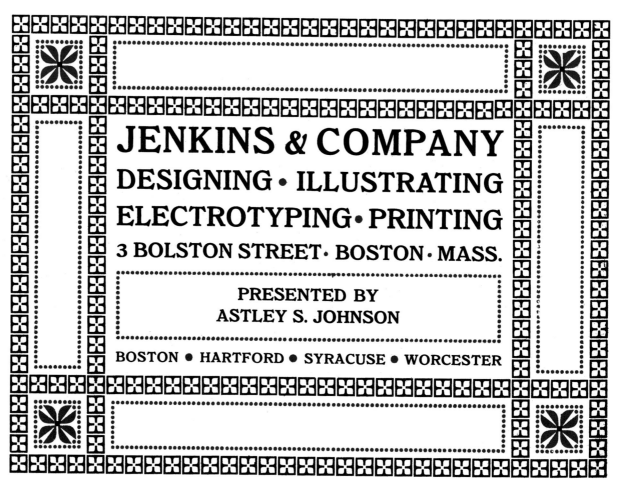

JENKINS & COMPANY
DESIGNING · ILLUSTRATING
ELECTROTYPING · PRINTING
3 BOLSTON STREET · BOSTON · MASS.

PRESENTED BY
ASTLEY S. JOHNSON

BOSTON · HARTFORD · SYRACUSE · WORCESTER

GRAFISCHE SIERKUNST

PROEVEN VAN MODERN
DRUKWERK VAN DE N.V
DRUKKERIJ DE PERS

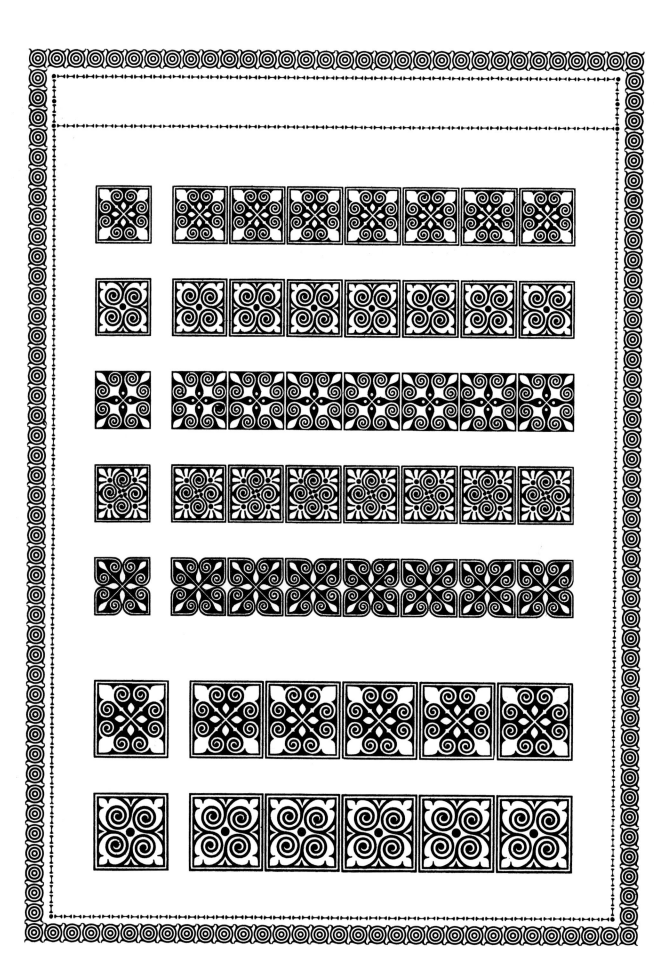

234

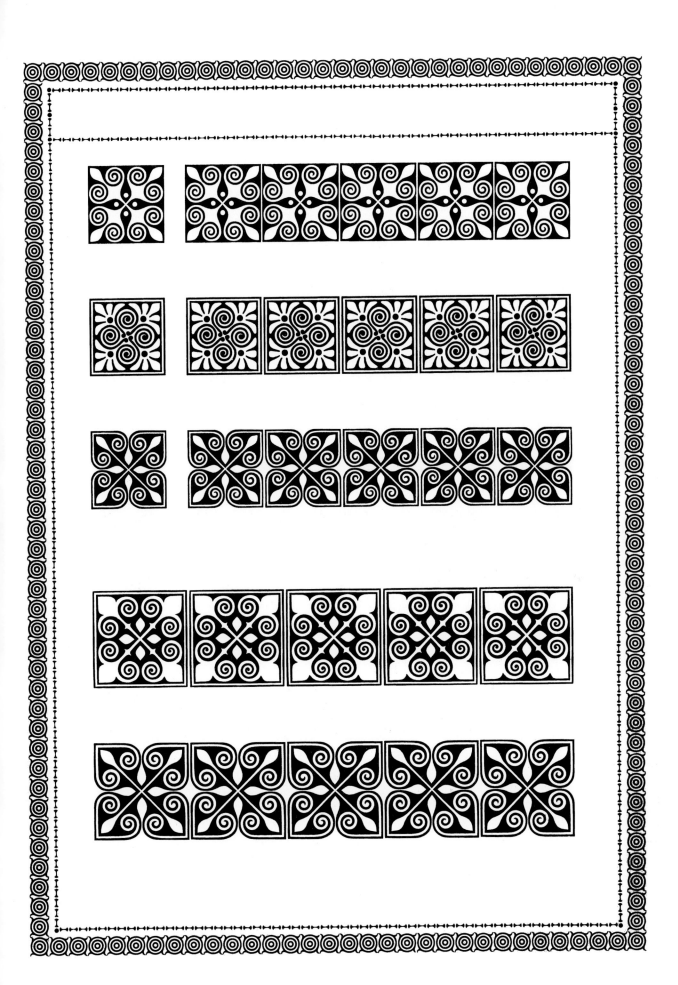

235

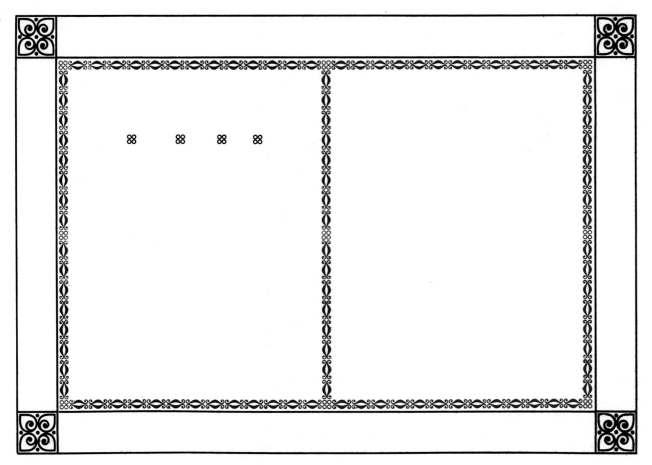

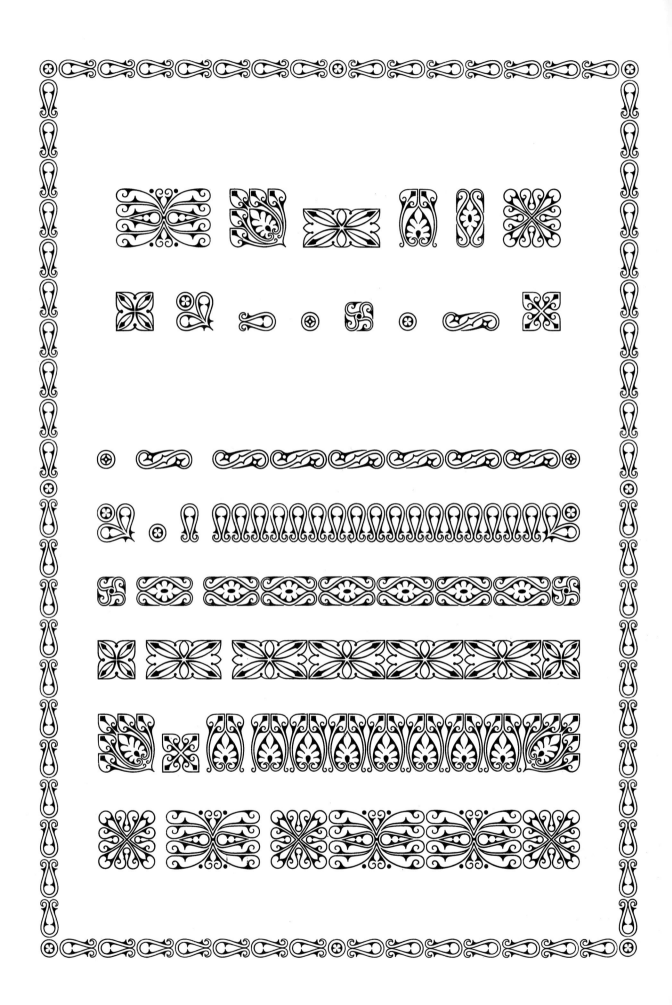

239

241

242

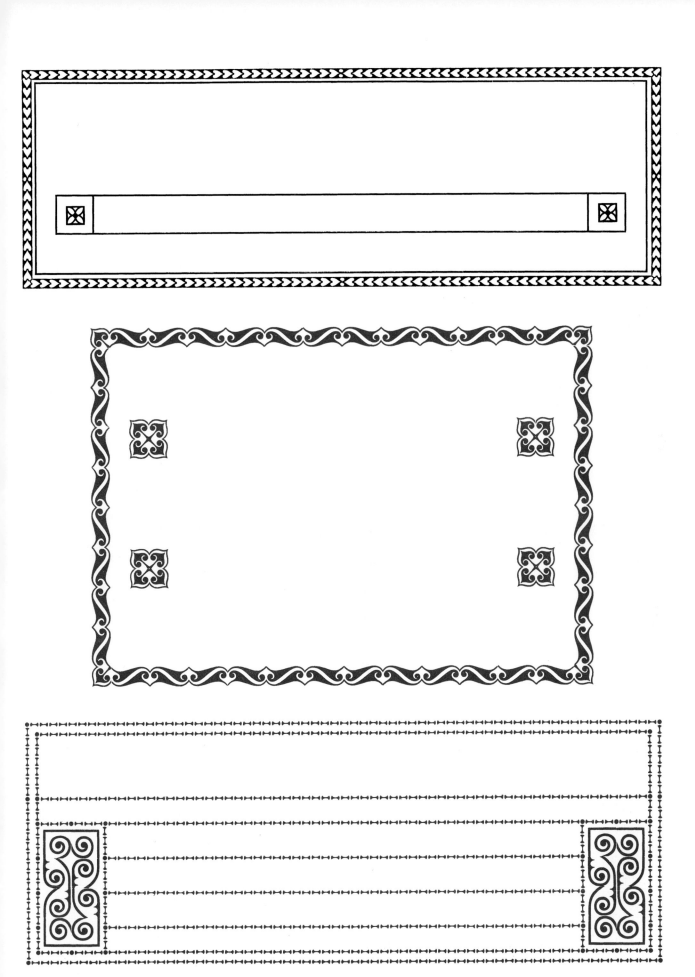

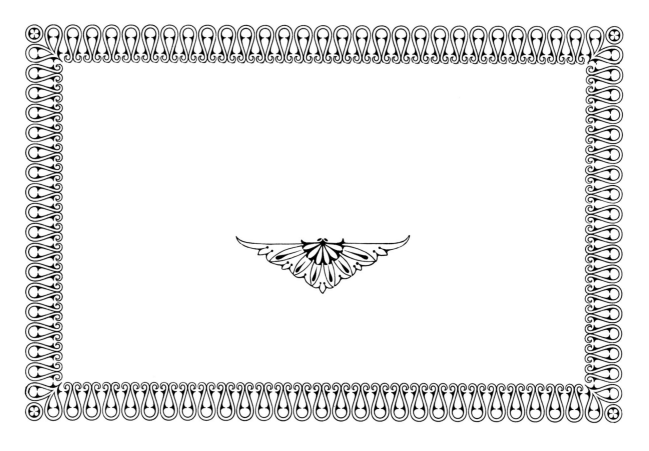

CHAPEAUX GARNIS

⊗

ANCIENNE MAISON

SPIER-BARNSTIJN

Weteringschans 251

Amsterdam

Tel. 8321

⊗

PRINTEMPS

PILSNER URQUELL

IMPORTEUR F. FISLTHALER
AMSTERDAM   ROTTERDAM

AUGUSTINER BRAU

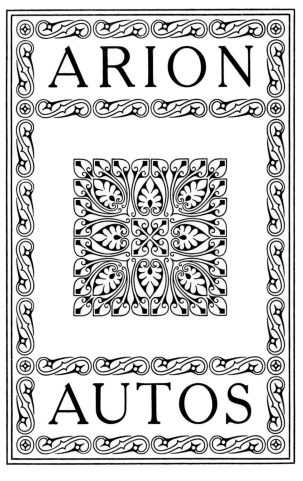

ARION

AUTOS

HOTEL
VICTORIA
PARIS

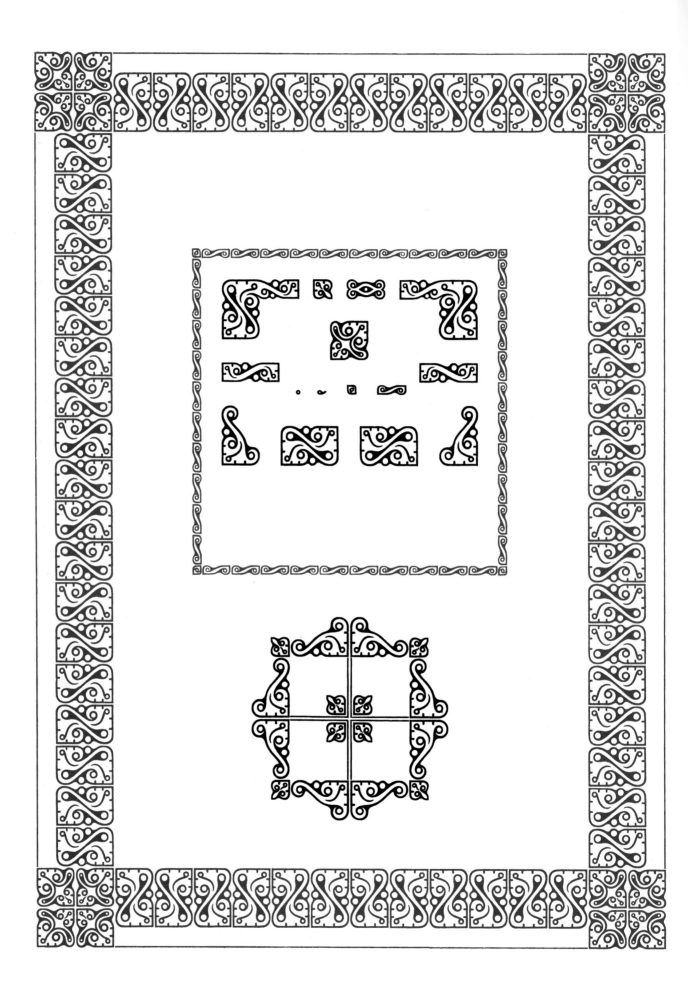

AGENDA
CALENDRIER
1915

HIRSCH & CIE
BRUXELLES

SAVOY HOTEL
VICTORIA EMBANKMENT
LONDON

THE FINEST HOTEL AND RESTAURANT
IN LONDON OVERLOOKING THE RIVER
⚘ AND THE EMBANKMENT GARDENS ⚘

251

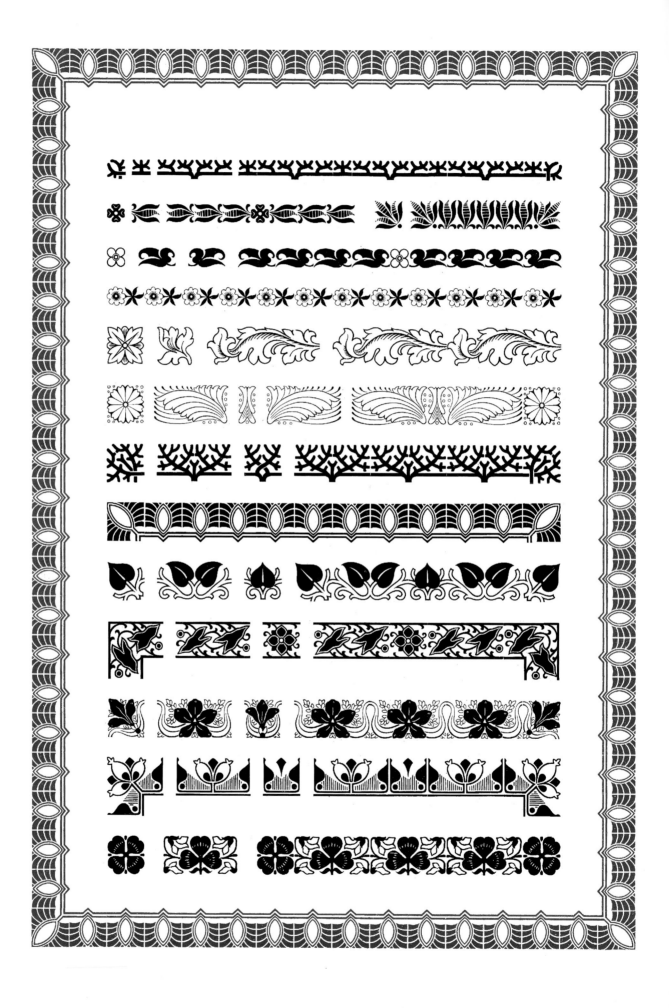

252

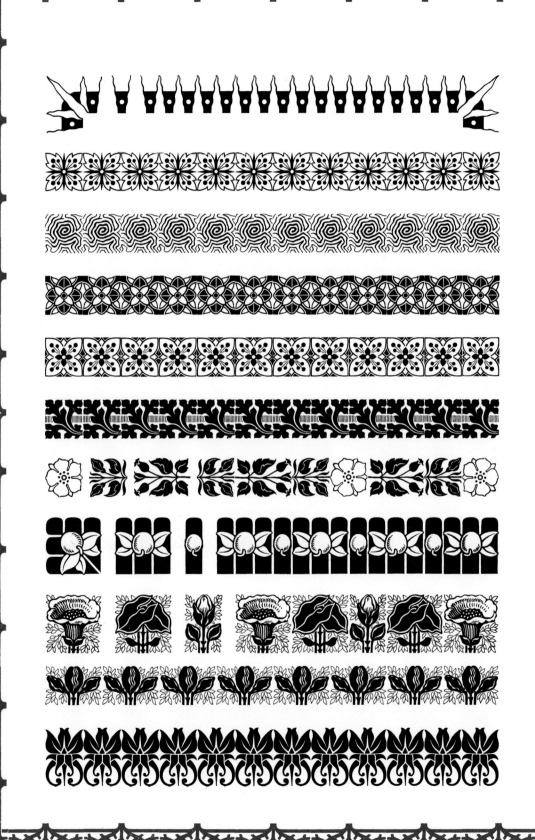

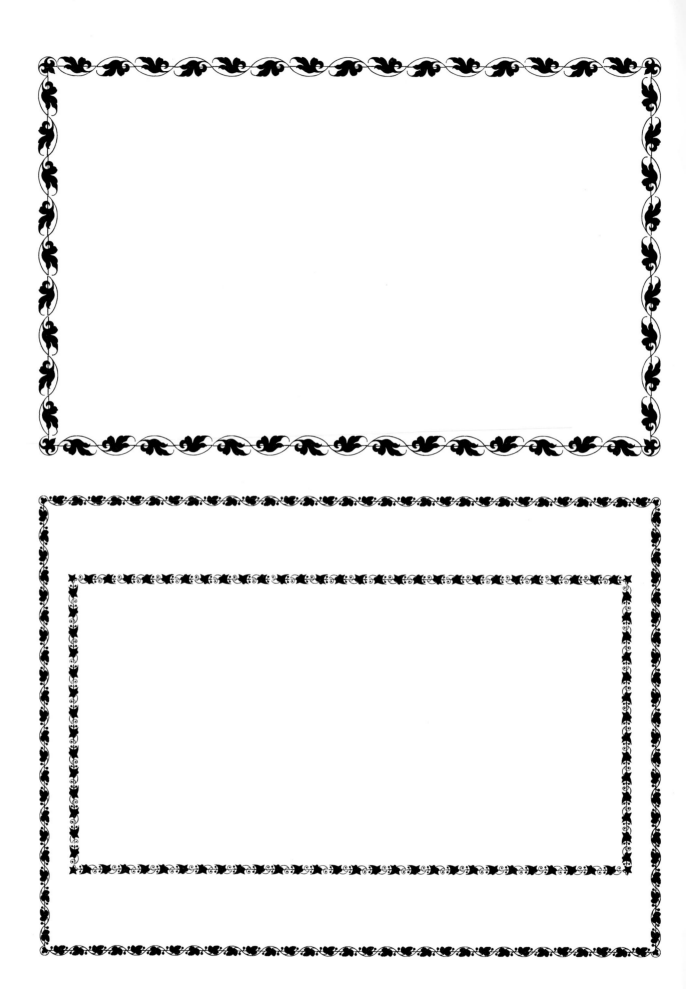

254

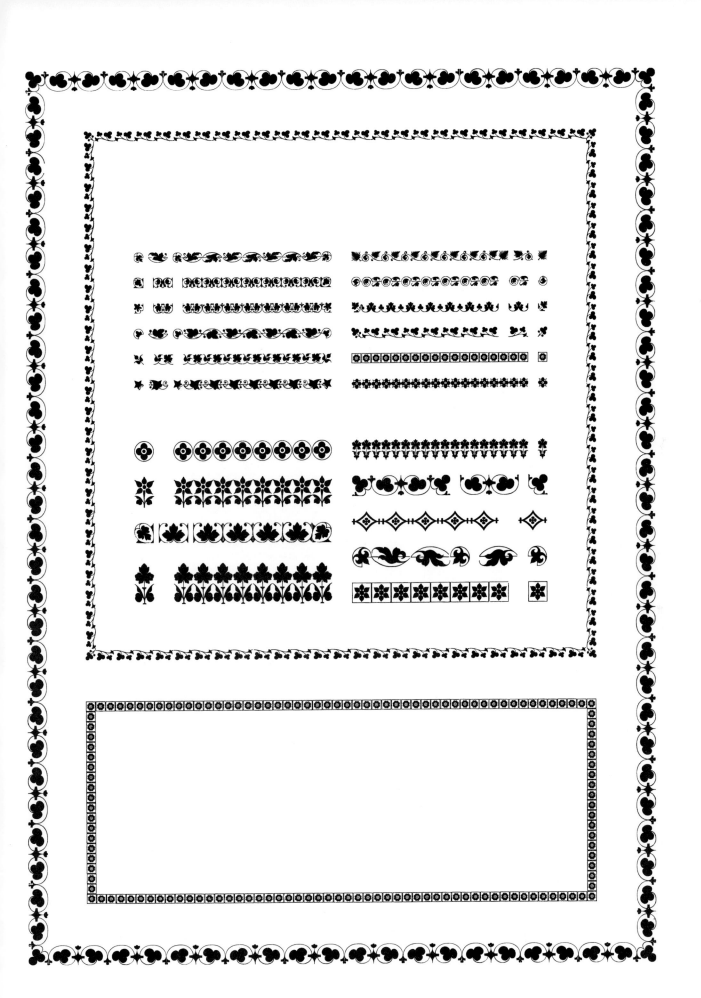

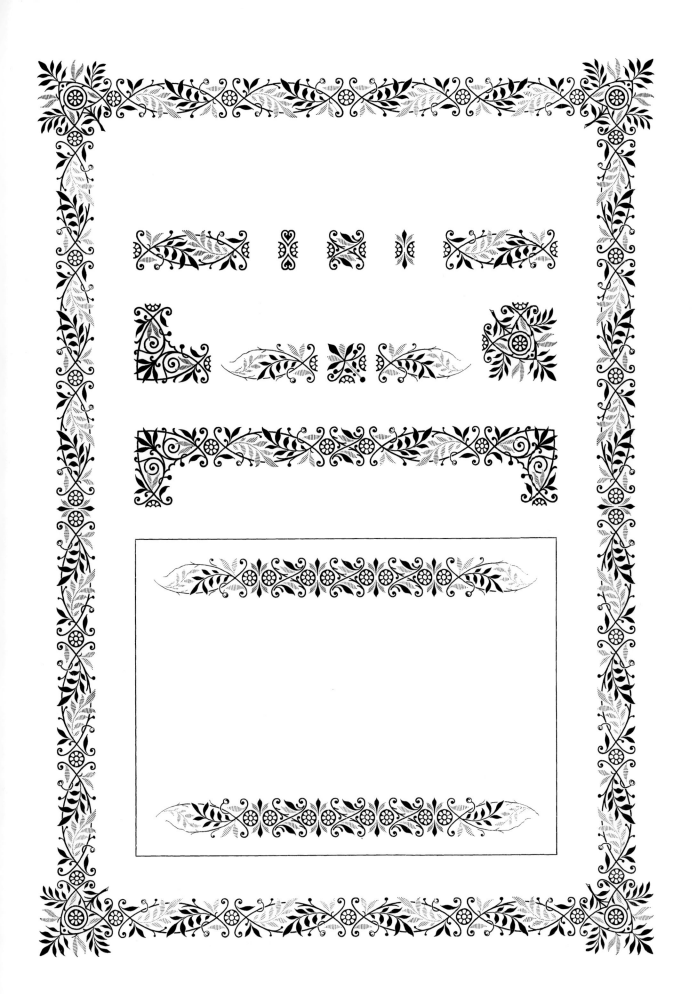

265

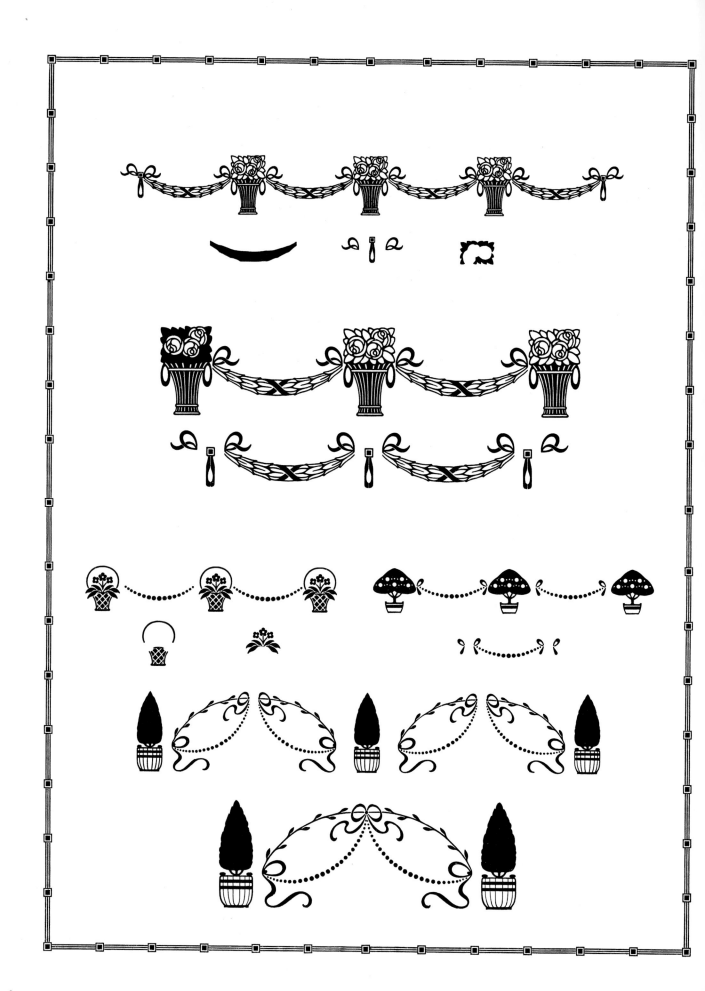

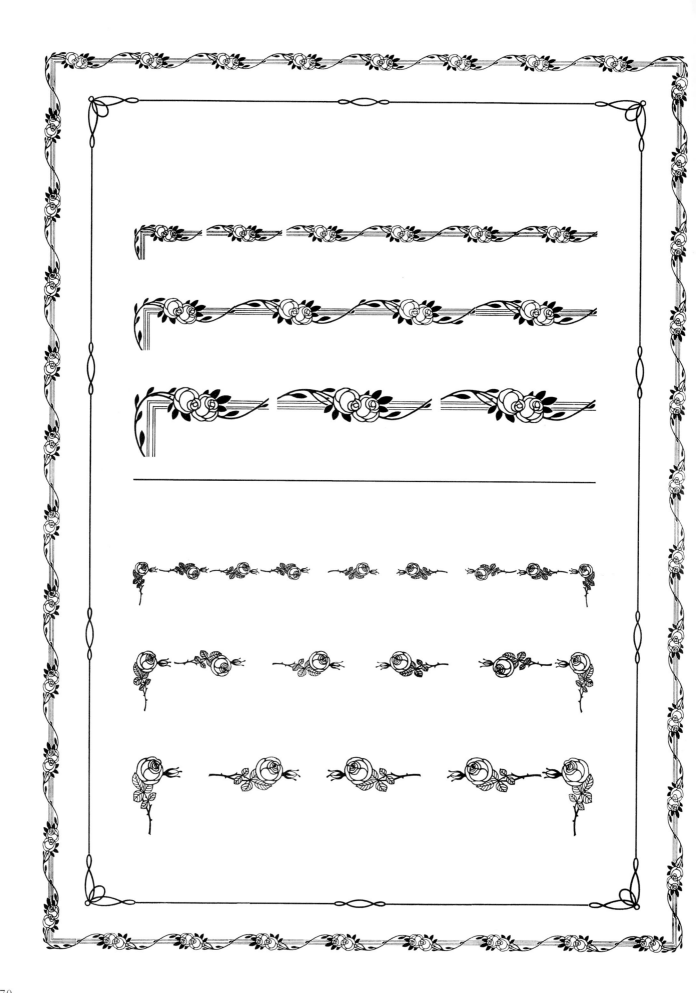

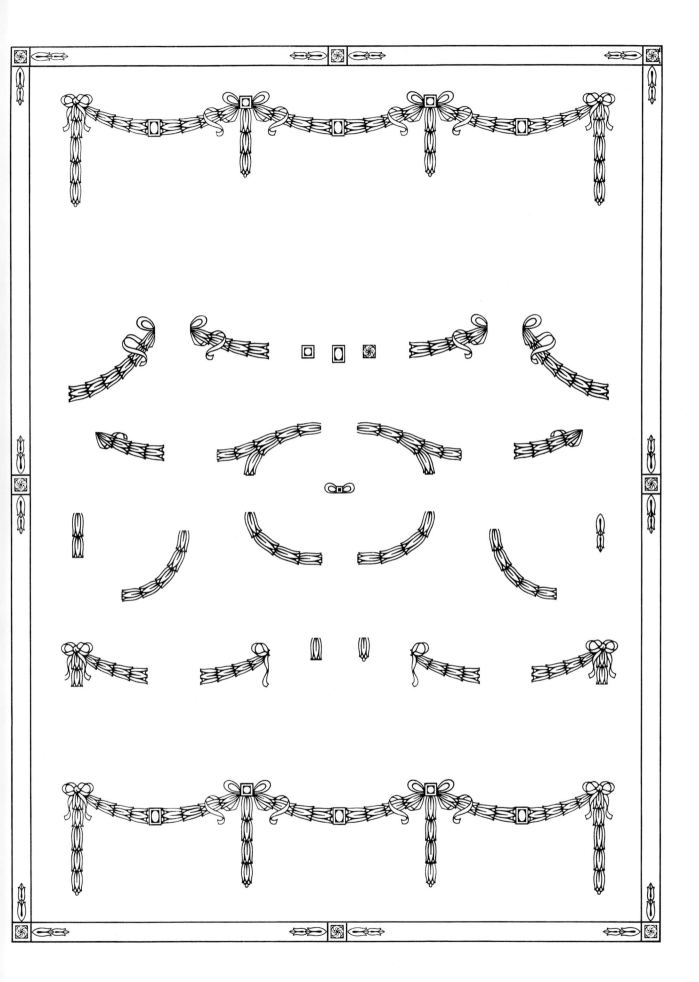

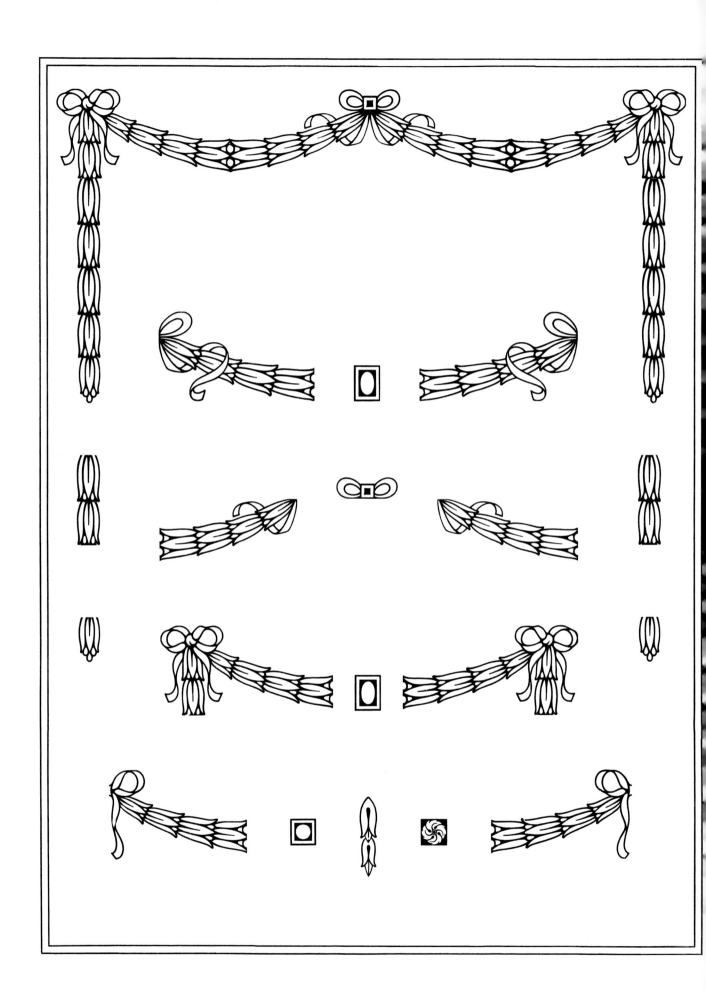

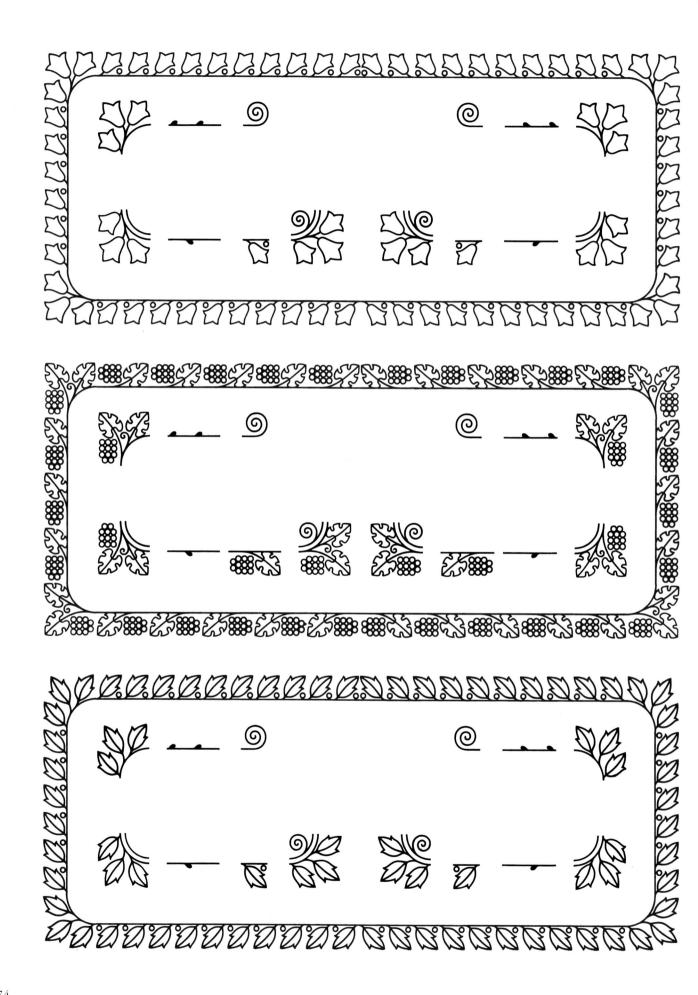

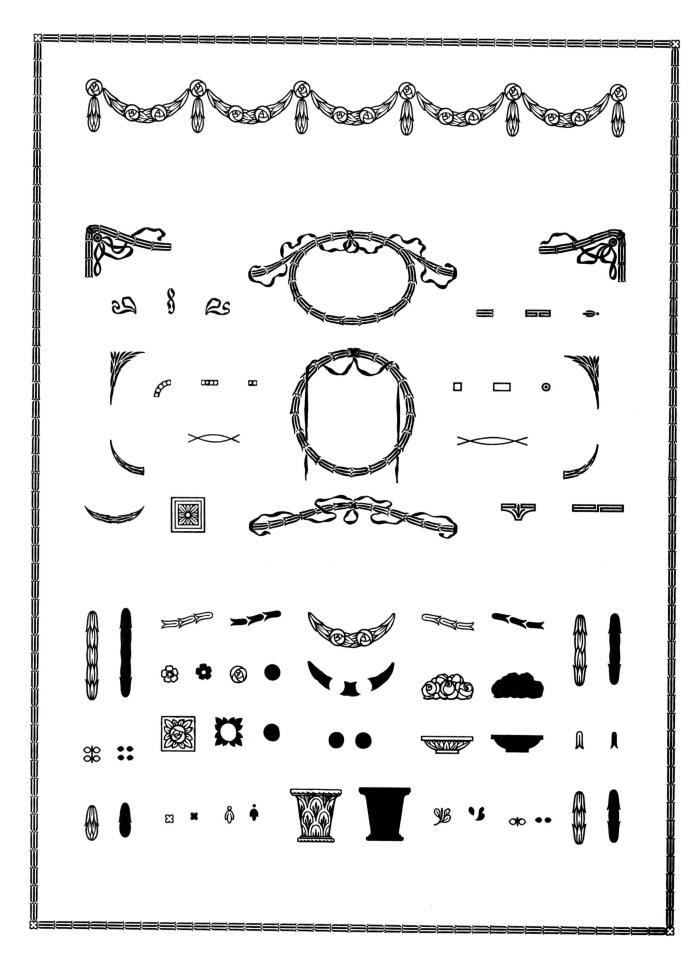

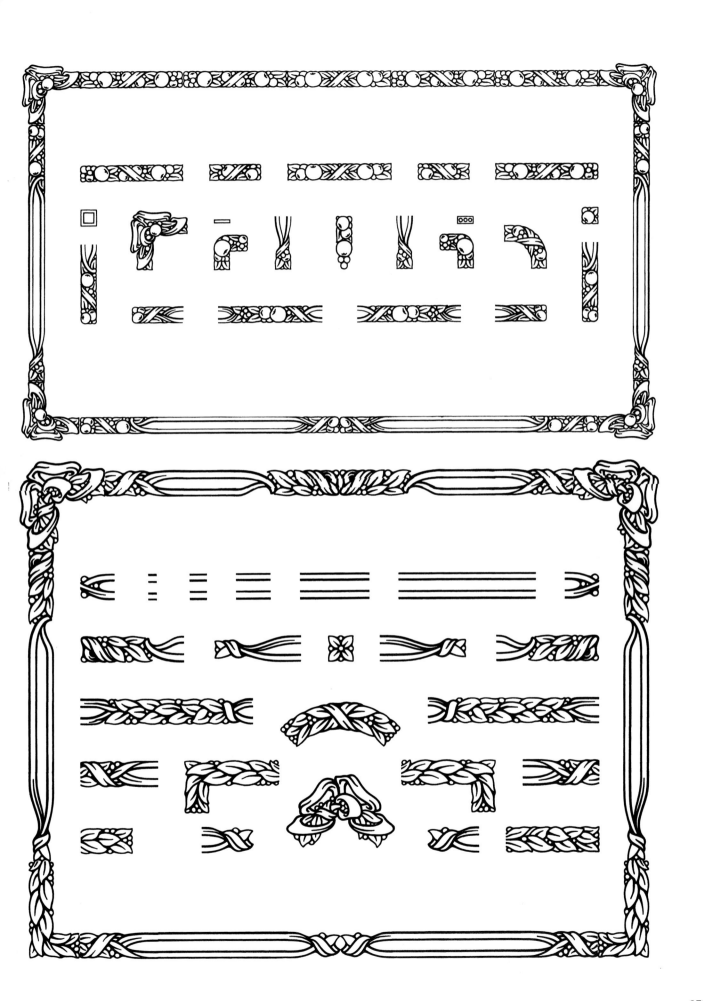

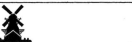

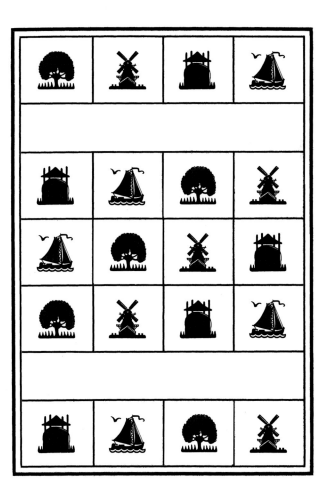

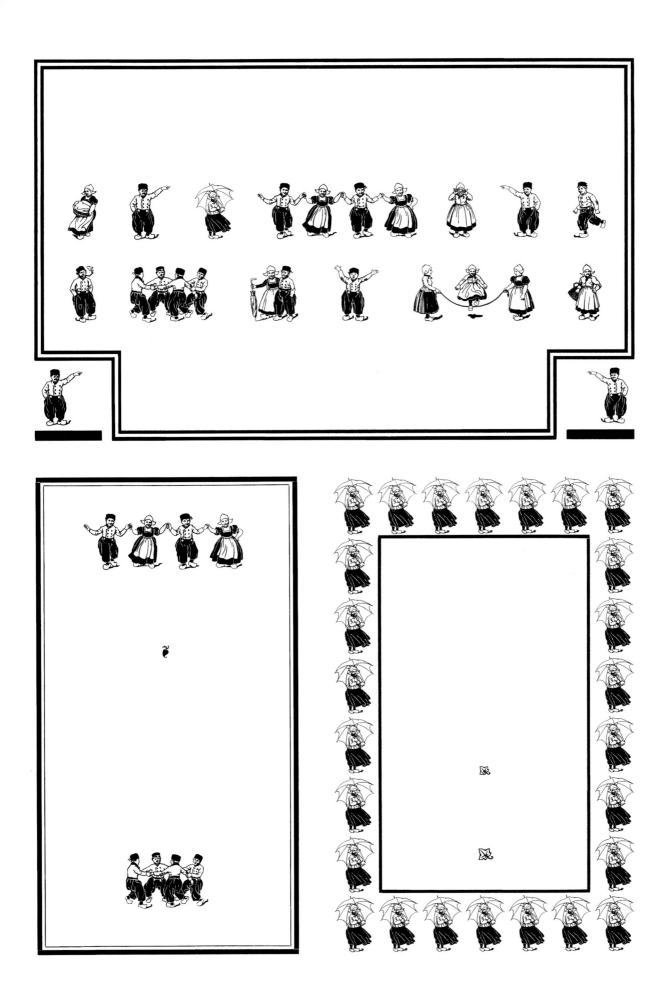

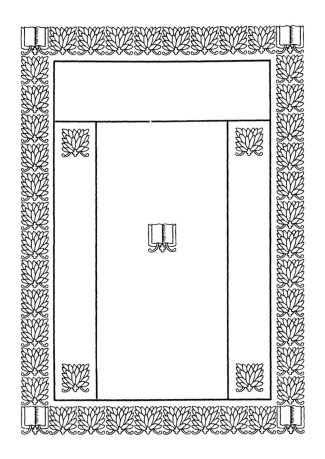

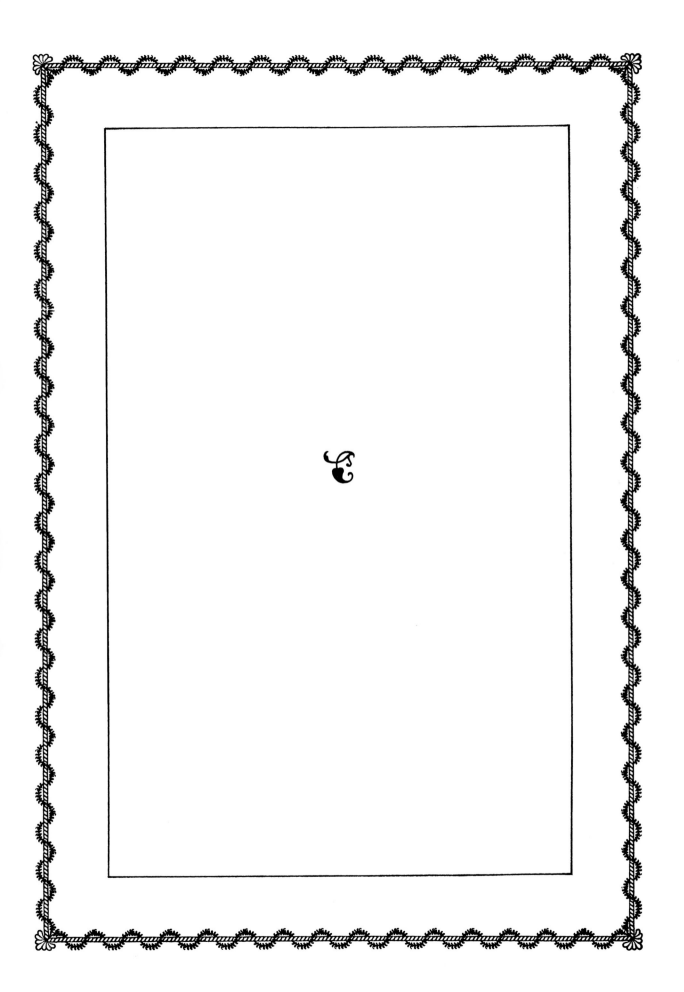

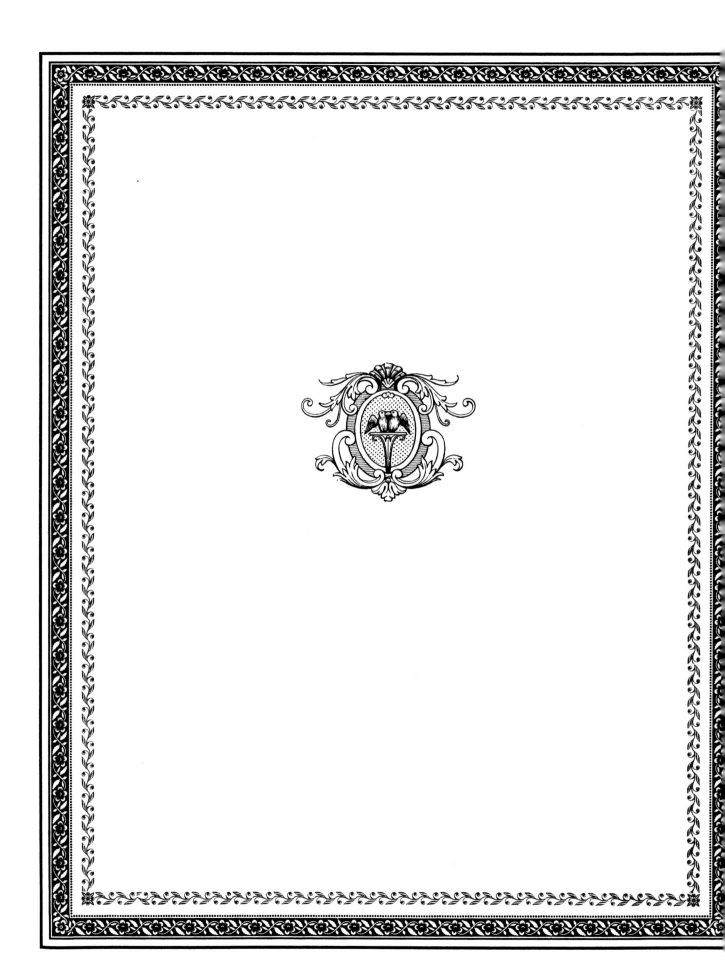

GRANDS MAGASINS

15, BOULEVARD DE LA MADELEINE

Exposition spéciale
des nouveautés
d'hiver

Lundi 21 Septembre
et les sept jours suivants

RESTAURANT · CAFÉ
L'EUROPE

BOULEVARD DU NORD · OSTENDE

PRENTEN

ontworpen of gegraveerd door

VROUWEN

benevens eenige

teekeningen

AMSTERDAM
BERNARD HOUTHAKKER
1913

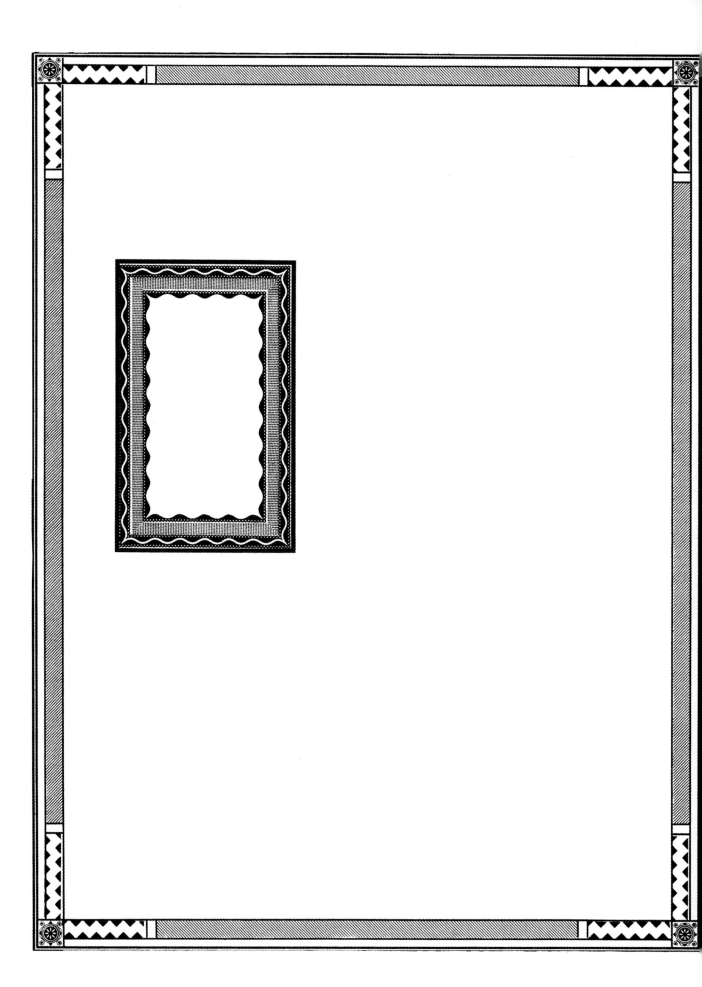

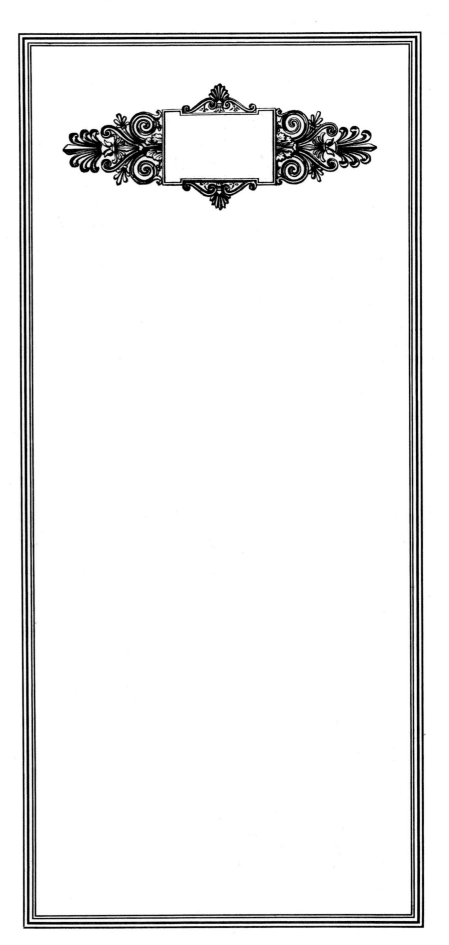

VIOLINS
ANCIENT OR MODERN

THE HISTORY
OF ANCIENT
VIOLINS AND
THE MODERN
METHODS OF
PRODUCTION

TYPOGRAPHICAL
DESIGNS

ORIGINAL SUGGESTIONS AND
REVIEW OF PRODUCTIONS OF
BRITISH PRINTER·CRAFTSMEN
PRACTICAL ARTICLES ON THE
LAY·OUT & COLOUR SCHEMES

THE TOWER
OF LONDON

BEING A STIRRING
ACCOUNT OF THE
FORT · DEPICTING
MANY EVENTS IN
ENGLISH HISTORY

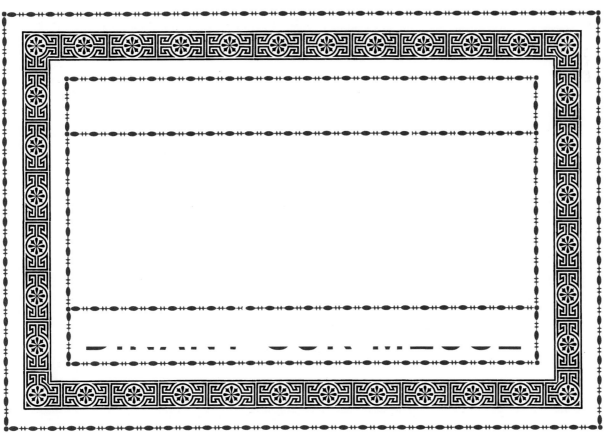

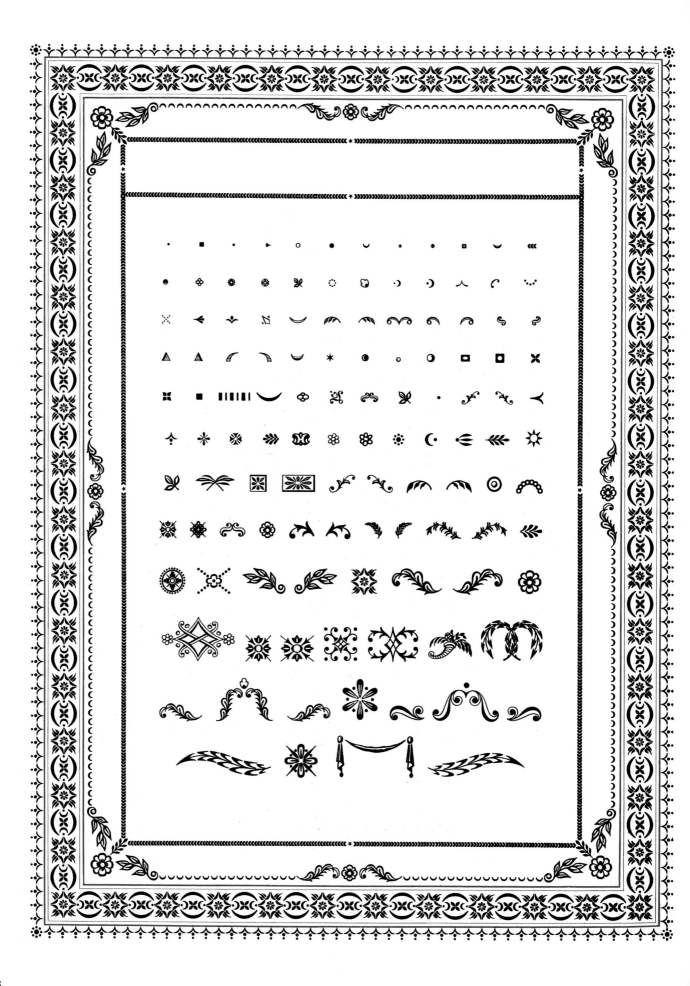

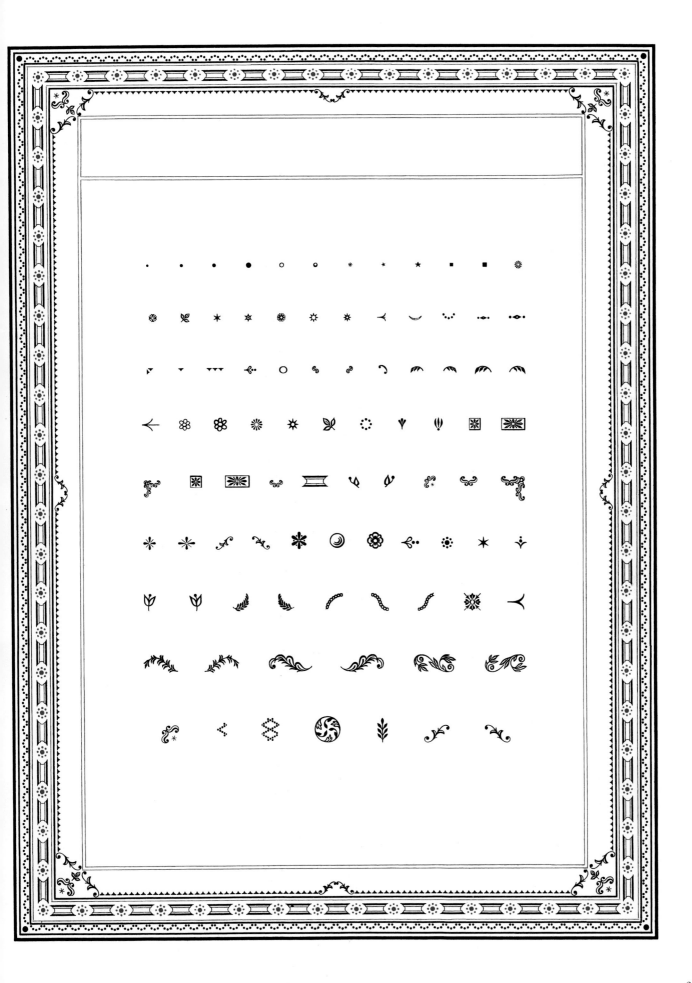

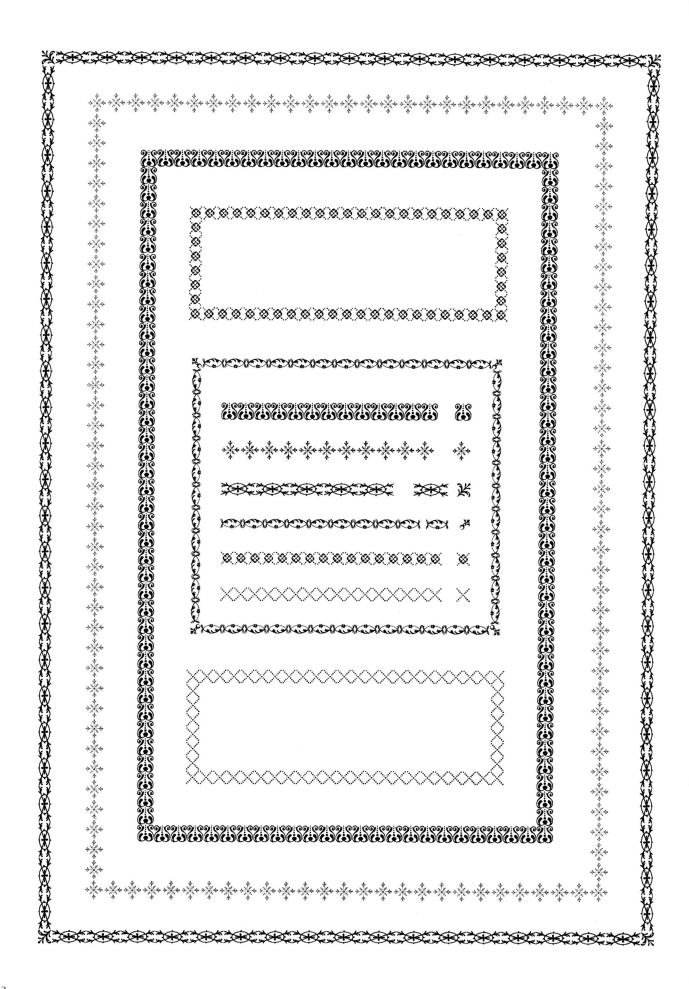

303

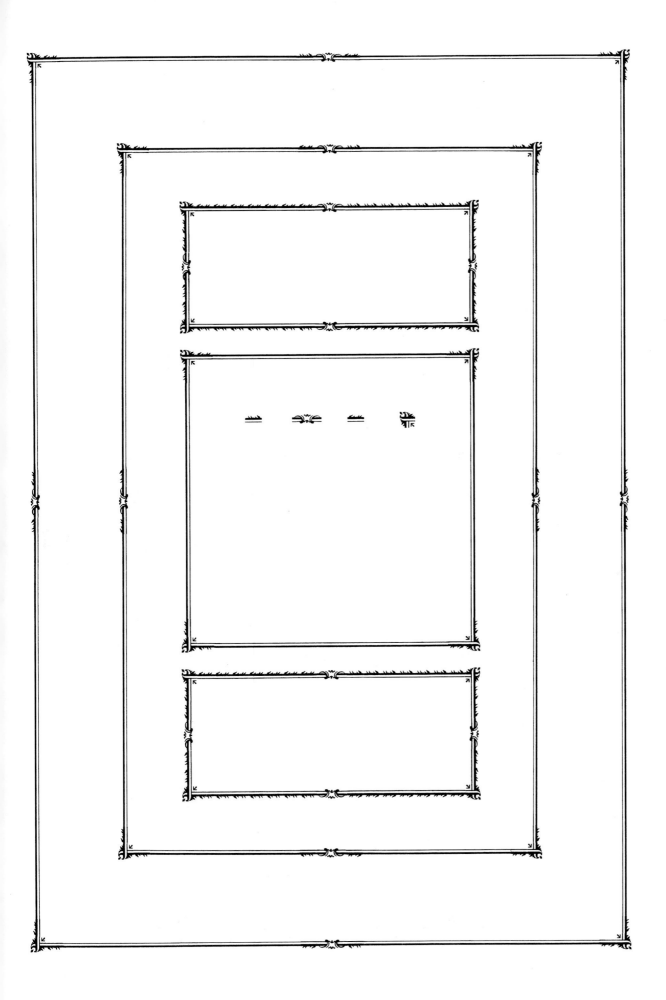

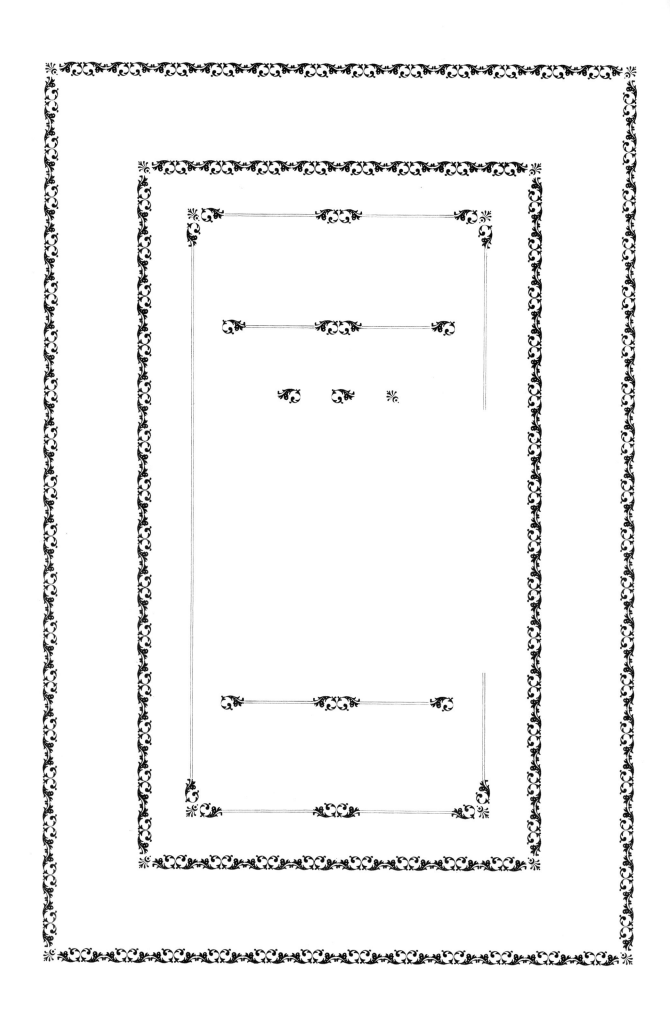

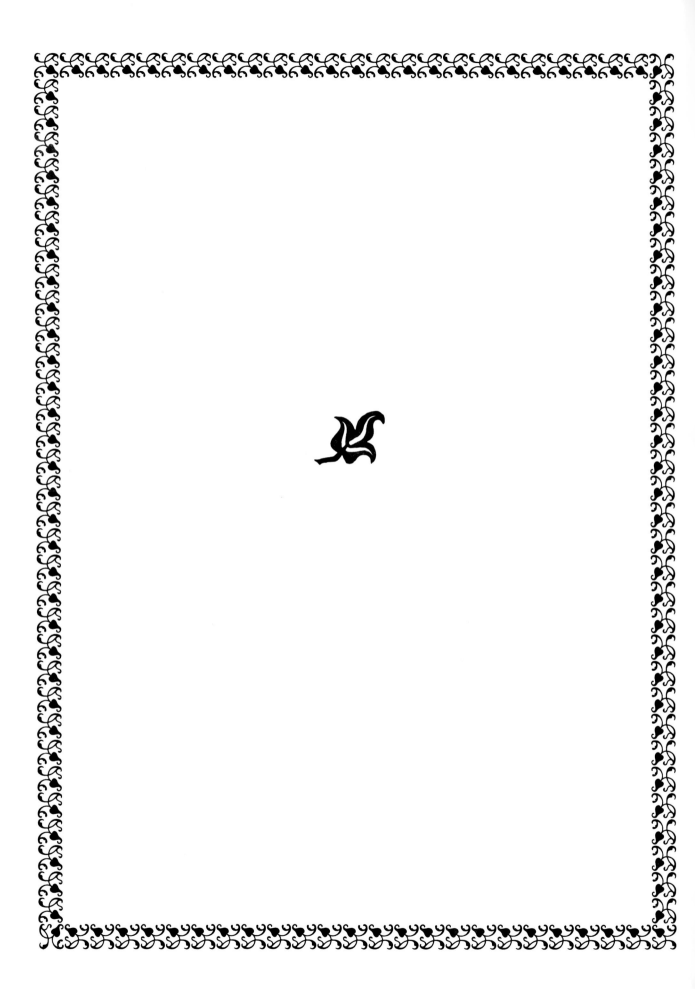

314

319

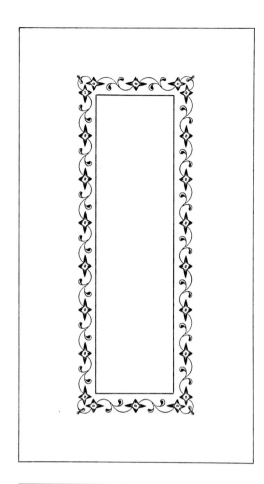

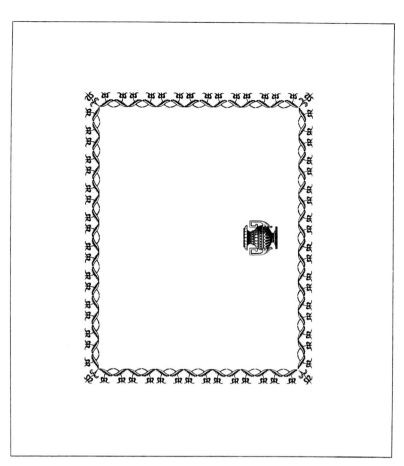

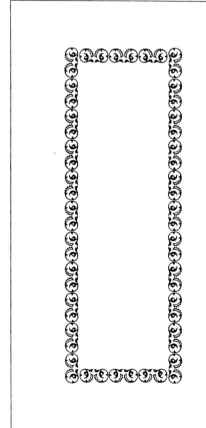

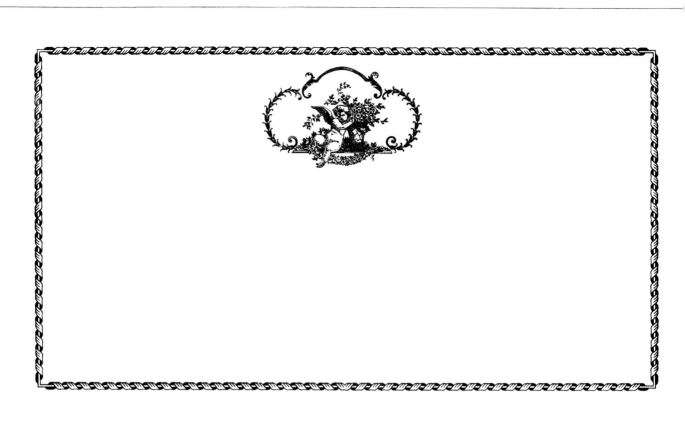

Kunstatelier Helios, Dresden-A.

Bronzen, Marmor-Skulpturen, Kamin-Uhren
Fayencen: Ginori, Wedgwood
Italienische Kunst-Gegenstände
Marmorsäulen, Schreibtischgarnituren, Rahmen
Elfenbein-Miniaturen

Stildekorationen berühmter Meister

Speisen-Folge

Schildkrötensuppe

Rheinlachs mit zerlassener Butter

Kalbsrücken mit Maronen
Lendenbraten

Straßburger Pasteten mit Trüffeln

Schnepfen und Salat

Kompott

Aufschnitt mit Butter

Obst

Fest-Essen

zu Ehren des

Mitteldeutschen Lehrer-
Sängertages

im Marmorsaal der Städtischen
Festspielhalle

Halle an der Saale

Pfingsten 1915

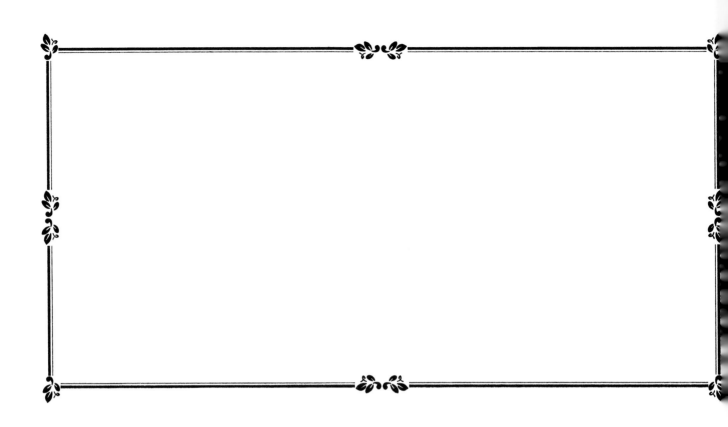

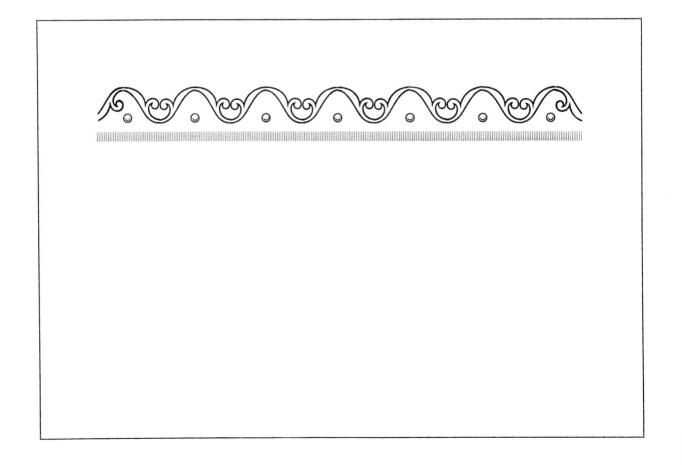

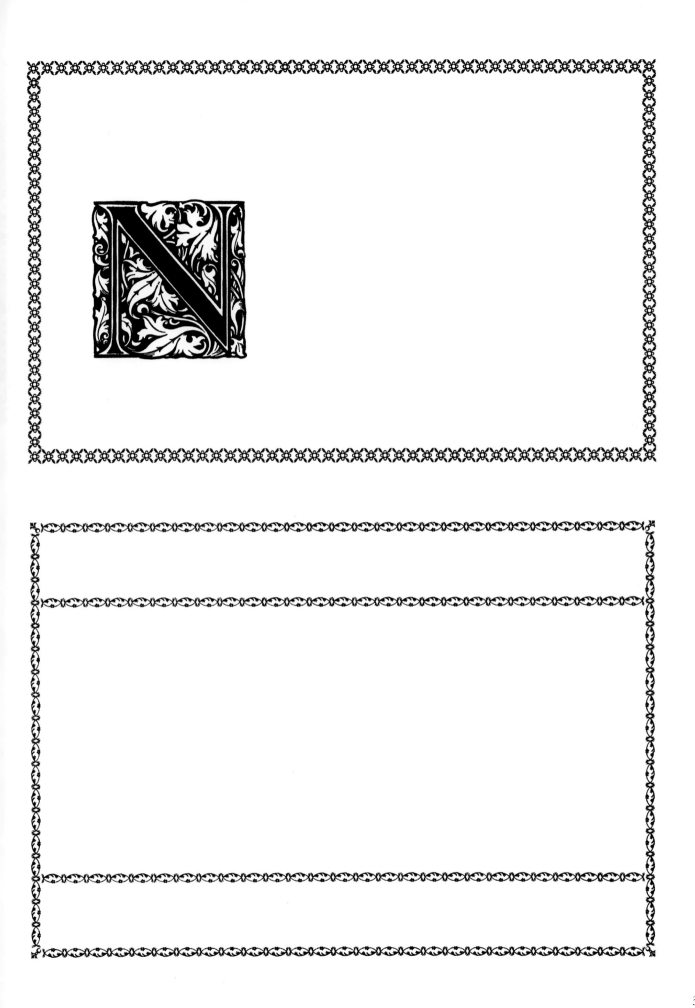

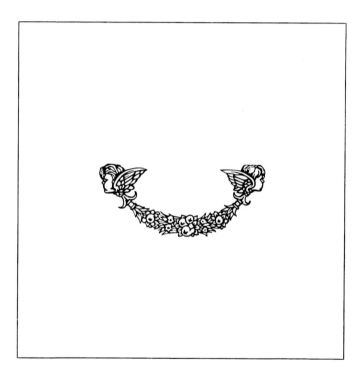

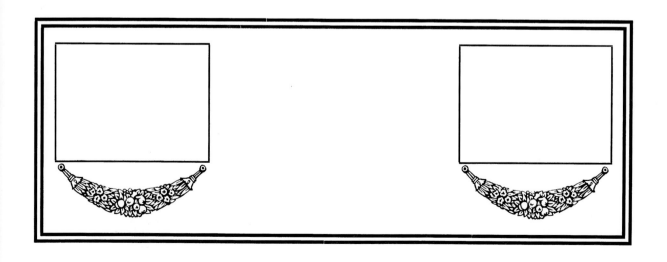

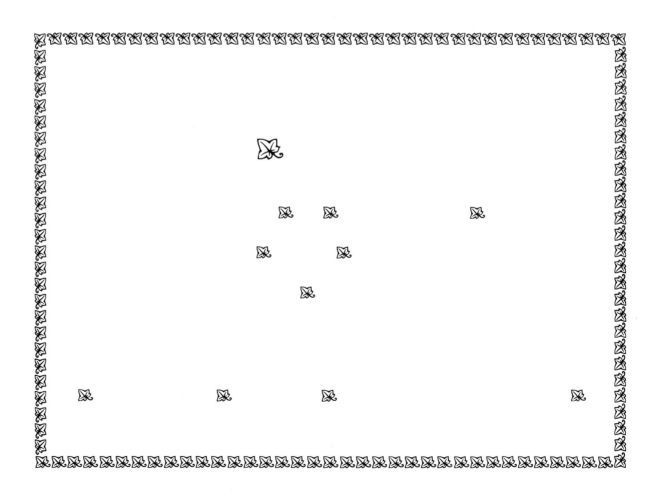

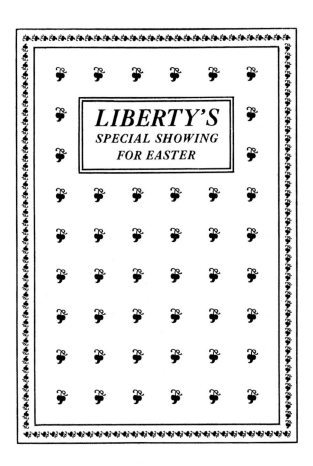

Programma

I

a. Soave sia il morir
Giovanni Pierluigi da Palestrina

b. Adoramus te
Paolo Agostini

c. O Domine Jesu Christe
Giovanni Gabrieli

II

a. Mein Freud' allein
Heinrich Isaak

b. Mach mir ein lustigs Liedelein
Hans Cristoph Haiden

c. Landsknechtständchen
Orlando di Lasso

Woensdag 13 Maart

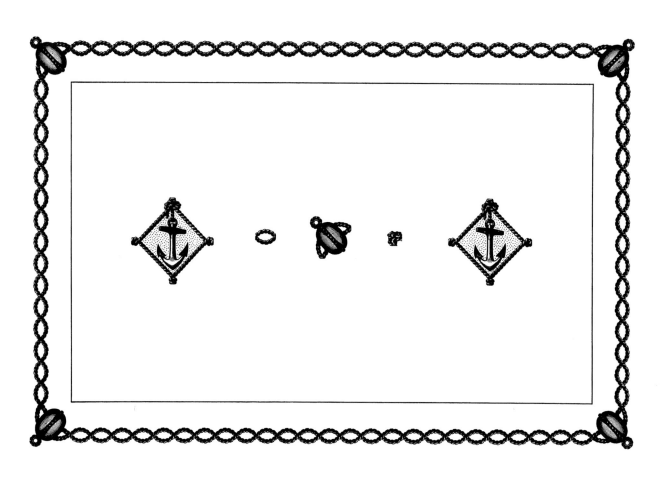

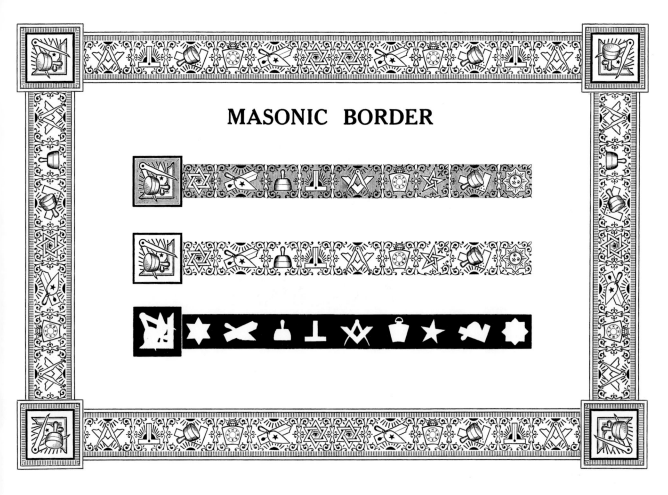

MASONIC BORDER

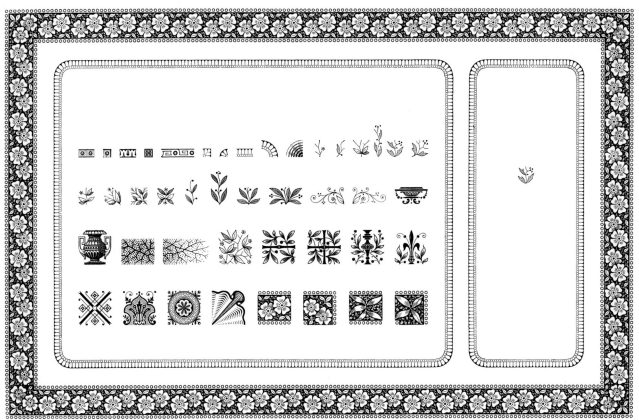

 **Smoking Corners**

 **EMBLEMATIC CORNERS**

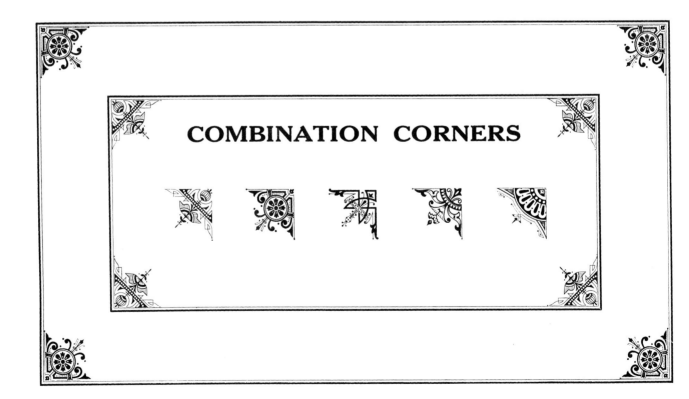

COMBINATION CORNERS

Classic Card Corners

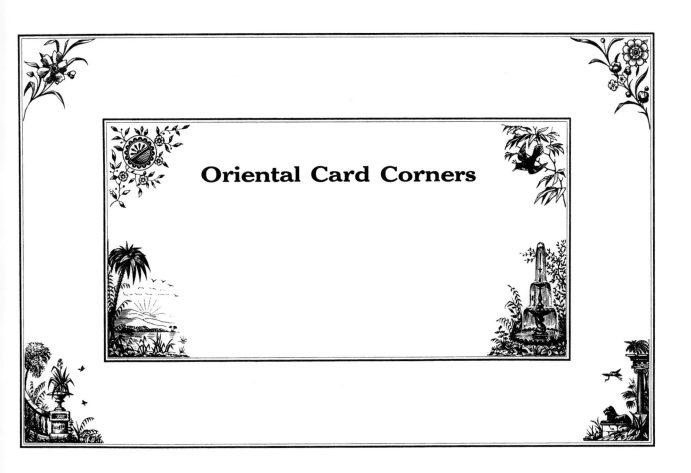

Oriental Card Corners

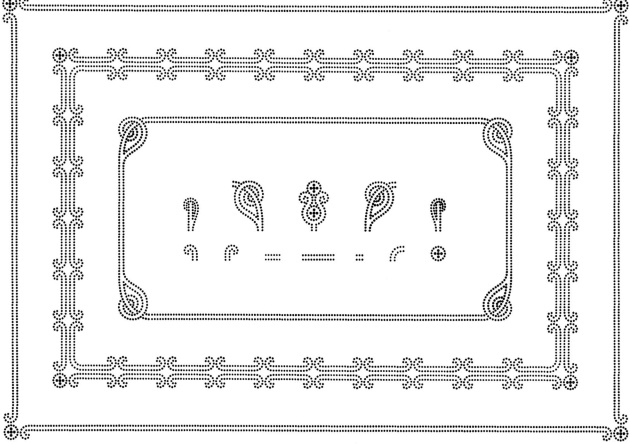

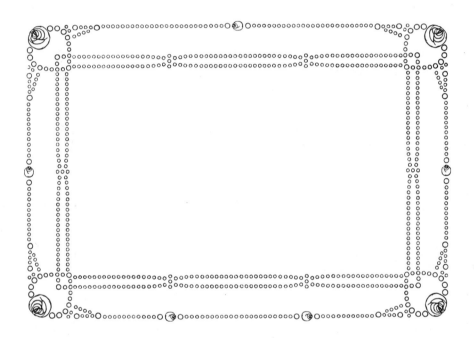

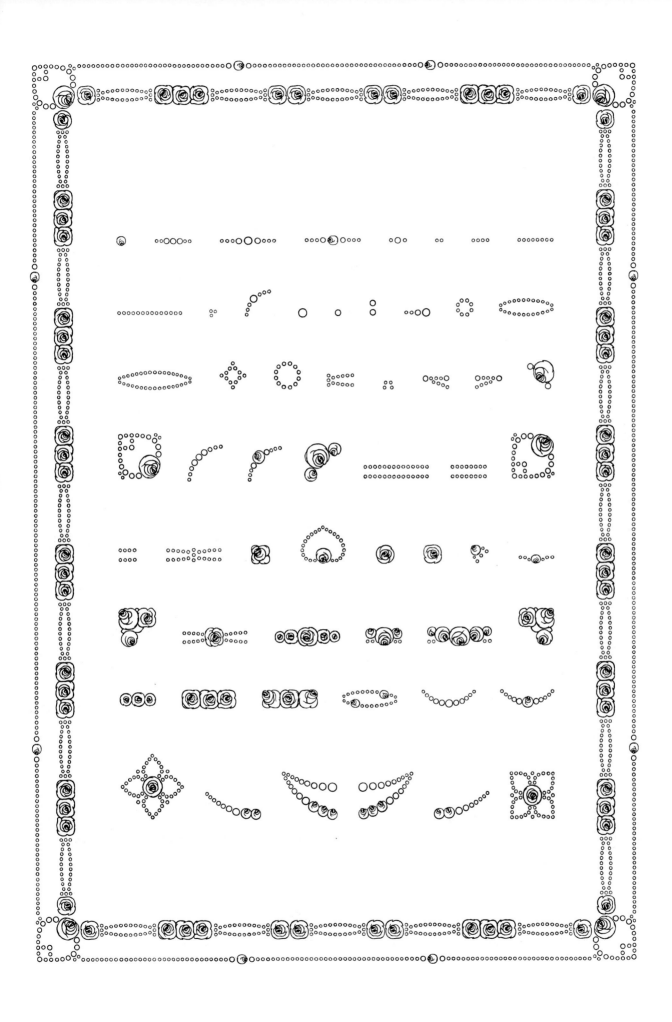

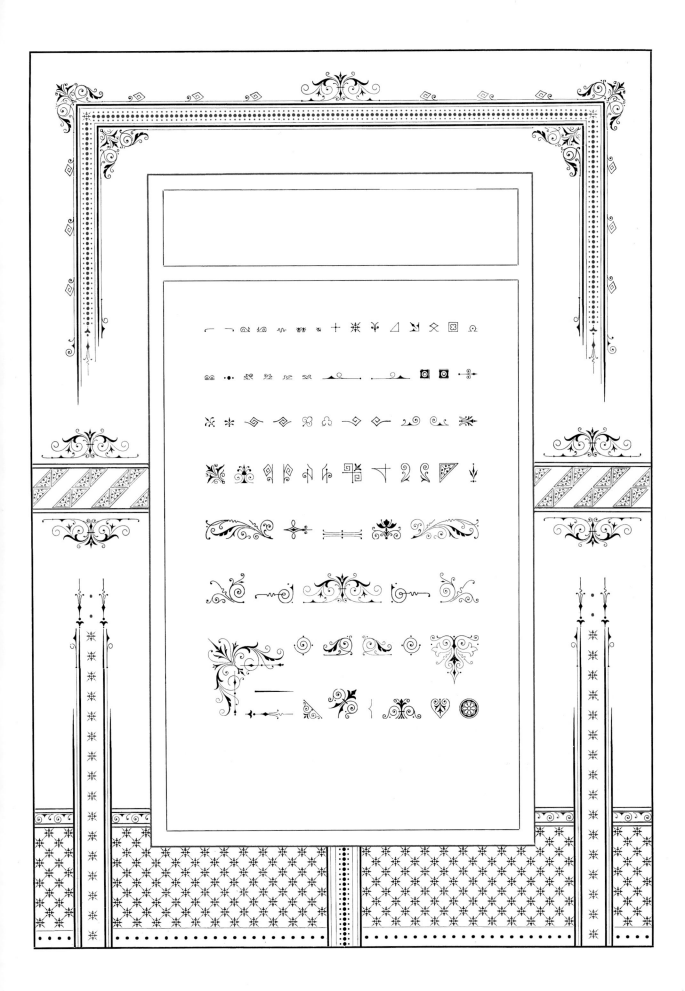

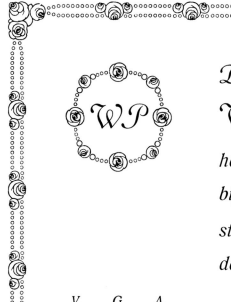

De Heer en Mevrouw

Van der Wulingen-Pourdonnelle

hebben de eer U hiermede uit te noodigen tot bijwoning van een avondfeest, dat zij zich voorstellen te geven op Donderdag 28 Februari, des avonds te 8 uur in „De Twee Steden"

's-Gravenhage, Kneuterdijk 35, 18 Februari 1914

V.　G.　A.
vóór 27 Februari a.s.

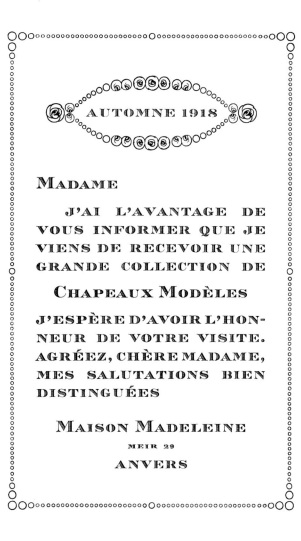

AUTOMNE 1918

MADAME

J'AI L'AVANTAGE DE VOUS INFORMER QUE JE VIENS DE RECEVOIR UNE GRANDE COLLECTION DE CHAPEAUX MODÈLES

J'ESPÈRE D'AVOIR L'HONNEUR DE VOTRE VISITE. AGRÉEZ, CHÈRE MADAME, MES SALUTATIONS BIEN DISTINGUÉES

MAISON MADELEINE
MEIR 29
ANVERS

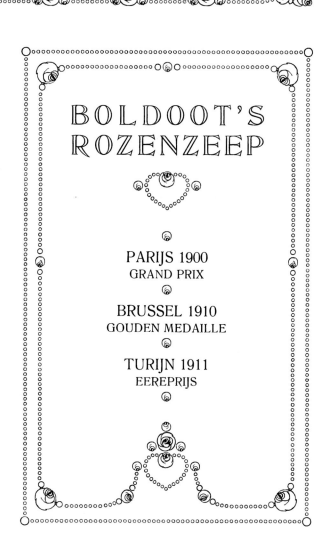

BOLDOOT'S ROZENZEEP

PARIJS 1900
GRAND PRIX

BRUSSEL 1910
GOUDEN MEDAILLE

TURIJN 1911
EEREPRIJS

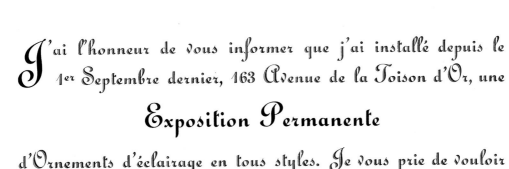

J'ai l'honneur de vous informer que j'ai installé depuis le 1er Septembre dernier, 163 Avenue de la Toison d'Or, une

Exposition Permanente

d'Ornements d'éclairage en tous styles. Je vous prie de vouloir bien me rendre visite à la première occasion et vous présente entretemps, M.................., l'assurance de nos sentiments dévoués.

Bruxelles, Octobre 1917   Emile Claeys Frères

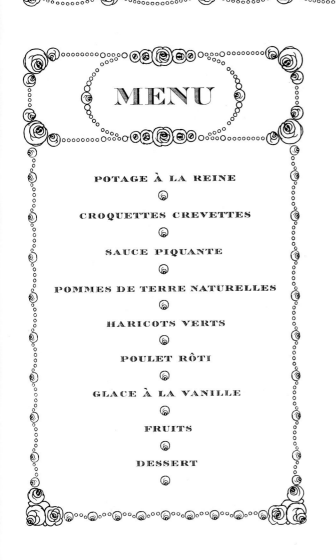

MENU

POTAGE À LA REINE

CROQUETTES CREVETTES

SAUCE PIQUANTE

POMMES DE TERRE NATURELLES

HARICOTS VERTS

POULET RÔTI

GLACE À LA VANILLE

FRUITS

DESSERT

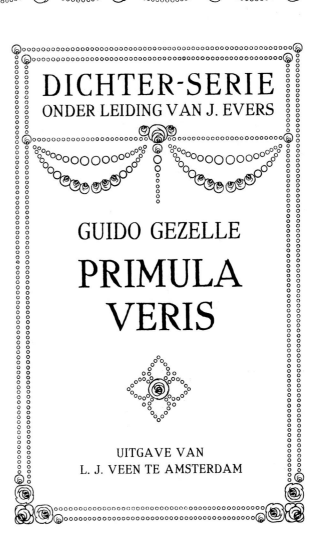

DICHTER-SERIE
ONDER LEIDING VAN J. EVERS

GUIDO GEZELLE

PRIMULA VERIS

UITGAVE VAN
L. J. VEEN TE AMSTERDAM

344

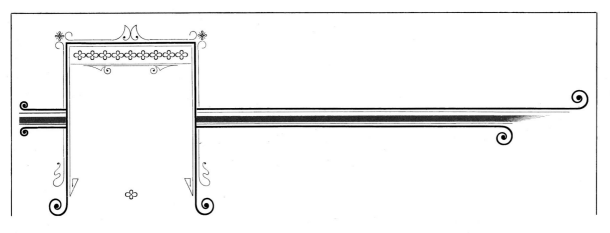

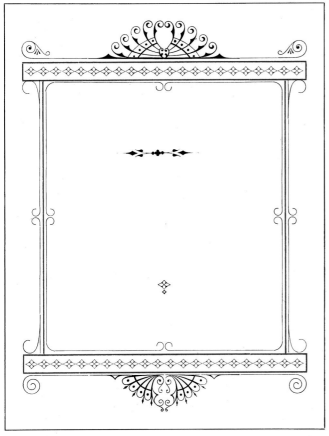

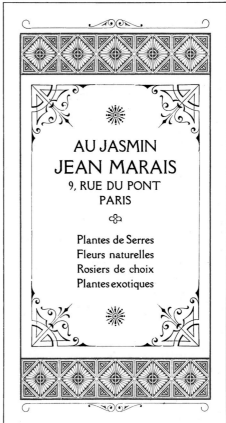

AU JASMIN
JEAN MARAIS
9, RUE DU PONT
PARIS

✤

Plantes de Serres
Fleurs naturelles
Rosiers de choix
Plantes exotiques

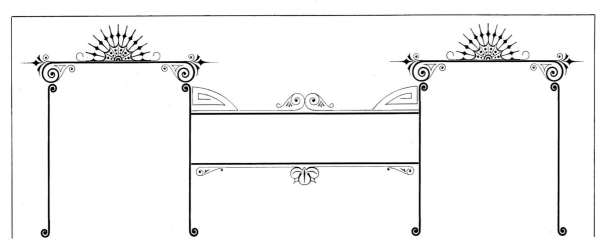

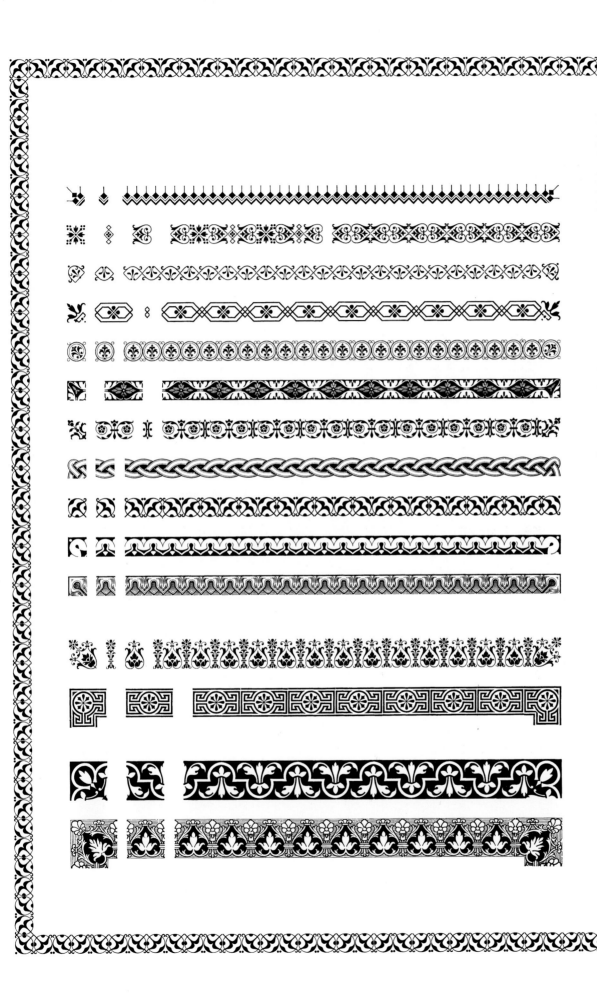

347

351

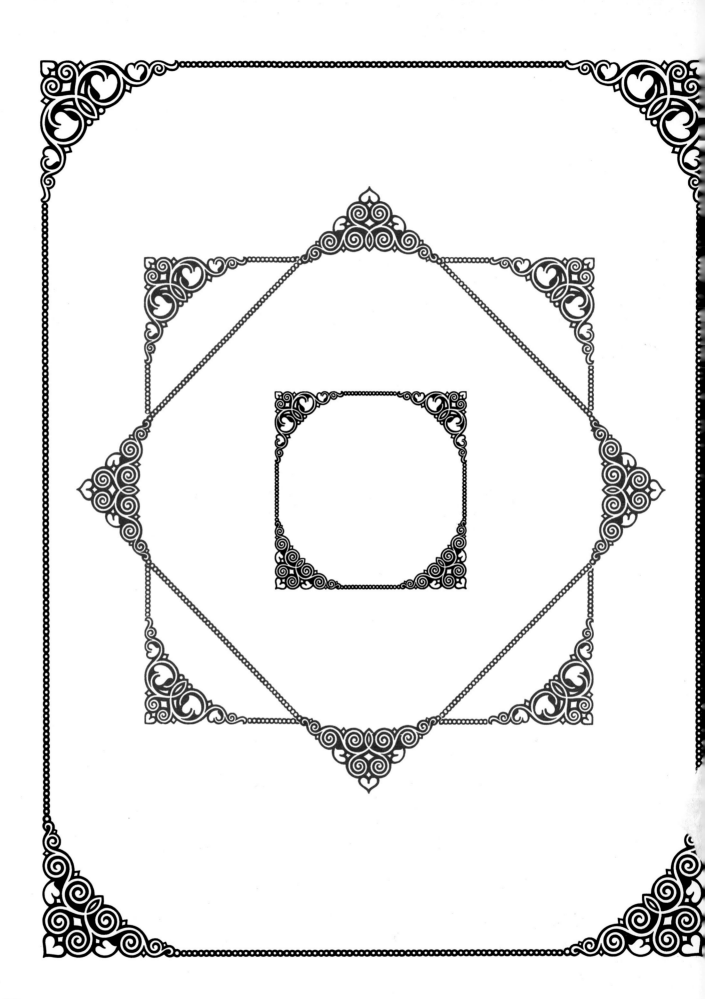